DOG DAYS ON ICE

Antarctic Exploration
in a Golden Era

Peter Noble

My best wishes

Peter Noble

Fids Errata (for those who know)

p9 & 23 Halley is of course west of Greenwich, oops!
p.45   Wensen had dark head with white triangle on
        forehead. Don't know how I got that wrong!
p.120   Accident was late 67 not early 68.
p.141   Stuart MacQuarrie not Chris Sykes
        (I got two journeys mixed up).

Peter

Published
by
Reardon Publishing
PO Box 919 Cheltenham
GL50 9AN England
Website: www.reardon.co.uk
Email: reardon@bigfoot.com
Tel: +44 (0)1242 231800

Written and researched
by
Peter Noble
Copyright © 2009

ISBN 1 873877 89 7
ISBN (13) 9781873877890

Design, layout and photographs
by
Peter Noble

Printed through
World Print Ltd

Dedication

For my children, grandchildren and all who want to know what it was really like in the old days, and what the old man got up to when he was a lad. But particularly for my wife, Jenny, who has enthused, relived the events with me, proofread and encouraged me throughout the preparation of this book.

Acknowledgements

To Halley Fids: Colin Wornham, Patrick Haynes, Tony Baker, Philip Cotton, Lewis Juckes, Bob Thomas, Geoffrey Lovegrove, Colin Johnson, Bob Lee, Edwin Thornton, Peter Witty, David Fletcher and Iain Campbell who provided much background information of their own and other expeditions.

To the many Fids who took part in the golden days and without whom I would have no story to tell.

Especially to Mike Skidmore with whom I dog sledged far and also Alan "Dad" Etchells with whom I tractored great distances - good companions both.

To British Antarctic Survey archivists Ellen Bazeley-White and Jo Rae, and glaciologist Hamish Pritchard for their generous assistance.

Finally to my old furry friends Whisky and the Hairybreeks for the many wonderful runs we had together.

Maps, Diagrams and Pictures

Poems, Rhymes and Songs

Why Now?

I surveyed the grey hair and balding heads, the lined faces, the stooped or halting walk of some, and the old protest song came to mind: "Where have all the young men gone?"

It was October 2006 and the British Antarctic Survey Club was celebrating fifty years of "Halley", the remote research base on the Antarctic continent. Along with four hundred other ex-Halley residents, I went along to the two day bun fight and chin wag noting the somewhat more luxurious accommodation than we had ever experienced "down south".

It was a wonderful gathering, meeting near forgotten friends, updating about what's happening in the twenty first century (that made us 1960s boys feel old!), but above all the inevitable reminiscences. As I listened and related my own stories, and particularly as I surveyed those ageing friends, I realised that in all too few years, an exciting and fascinating period of British exploration was to be forgotten.

True, there is an extensive archive at the British Antarctic Survey offices in Cambridge, but virtually all of this consists of formal reports; little is recorded about day to day living at Halley, of the now extinct experience of working with dogs, of camping on long expeditions, of the cold, of how it all affected the men who lived there. My own time and work at Halley had built on the efforts and dedication of those who established and maintained the base in the years before our cohort arrived; and particularly on those who undertook the many early field trips.

I was destined and privileged to work with the huskies, those lovely animals that featured prominently in explorations at Halley for scarcely a decade. From the humble beginnings of "Stumpy", the base pet in 1958, an importing and breeding programme was started in 1962 that produced a peak of 69 animals (adults and pups) in 1968 but by 1972 huskies had been internationally declared an "alien species" and should be discontinued. I leave it to the reader to imagine what discontinued meant. A couple of dogs, demoted once more to base pet status, managed to survive the decade but the great days of dog travel were over. That other alien species "man" with his increasingly polluting tractors and aircraft was however deemed essential, but one is left whimsically wondering how many billion husky farts equals one minute of a jet engine exhaust!

The 1960s were I believe the golden age of exploratory expeditions undertaken by the British Antarctic Survey and this book presents a personal account of an amazing, exciting and life changing experience.

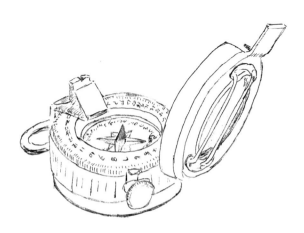

1   Leavings

"Time to go", I mused without enthusiasm. With a strange growing reluctance I shouldered my rucksack and gave a final, checking and nostalgic glance around my bunk room. This little seven foot square box had been my sleeping quarters for most of the past two years and small though it was, I shared it with another member of the base personnel, but he being twenty stone something, and an ex-wrestler, meant that I always slept on the top bunk. Still, it had had its advantages: occasional morning tea in bed and a supreme feeling of security. Not that personal security was an issue but our bunks were certainly well anchored at night. We had got the place looking homely too.   Alan Smith, "Big Al" as he was affectionately known, was a skilled carpenter and builder and I was learning the trade of   electrician.   I could also assemble flat-pack Ikea-type furniture without diagrams long before Ikea was itself unpacked. Yes, our room looked pleasant, quite comfortable really, with its varnished timber bunks, tastefully painted two tone wardrobe (the colours carefully selected from the vast range of four available). The *pièce de résistance* however was the rear wall with its display alcoves and hidden lighting. Well, it would all be someone else's now, to reconstruct or redecorate as required. In their turn they would make their home 75° south and 26° east at this British Antarctic Survey station "Halley Bay", and after them, others would come, and then others. There would always be a stream of enthusiastic young men (it was just men in those days) keen to commit themselves to a couple of years isolation on the Antarctic continent, keen, gullible young men just like I had been.

I recalled with a wry grin the time I first met the boss, Sir Vivian Fuchs, director of the British Antarctic Survey or BAS as it was always known thereafter. I was sitting in an office at the old headquarters of the Survey No. 30 Gillingham Street in London. It had been several months since I had applied for a post with BAS but had heard nothing and I had resigned myself to another year teaching fourteen year olds who didn't want to be taught. Then the letter arrived inviting me to interview. I was so naive I knew nothing about interview technique, about researching the job or the company beforehand, and there I sat in front of the great Sir Vivian and his colleague Bill Sloman. No doubt I was asked various questions about my limited career to date, my climbing, my teenage expeditions, but then I do recall the questioning turning to Antarctica.

"And what do you know of the Survey, Mr Noble?"

"Not very much," I admitted

"Do you know how long we British have been operating in Antarctica?"

I had heard of Captain Scott so guessed that that was the commencement. Sir Vivian looked at Bill and tried another tack.

"Do you know how many bases we have in Antarctica? or how many men are down there?" The double barrelled question implied that he expected a negative answer. He got one. In desperation he asked, "Do you know where the British operate?" Now here I was lucky. On the wall behind Sir Vivian was a large map of Antarctica that clearly showed the South Atlantic and knowing that the British tended to do everything on a shoe string and stiff upper lip, I guessed that the bases would be as close to the UK as possible to save on transport. I pointed vaguely to the Antarctic Peninsula and the Weddell Sea, due south of the Atlantic. Both men heaved sighs of relief.

"And do you still want a job with the Survey?" asked Bill Sloman.

My enthusiasm was as gushingly positive as my knowledge was dismally negative - and I got the job!

I grinned again at the thought of that interview, Sir Vivian had got what he wanted too: a keen, ignorant, malleable recruit who would tackle anything as an honour! Someone who could be moulded and made into something useful. Well, that had certainly happened when I considered the many skills I had acquired and responsibilities I had taken on as a General Assistant or GA as I would be known. More importantly I had joined the brotherhood of "Fids".

In 1962 the Falkland Islands Dependancies Survey matured into the British Antarctic Survey but for many of the "old guys" the organisation retained its acronym "Fids". Inevitably those who worked for the Survey also became known as fids with the obvious singular form of "fid". The title had to be earned however and the earning required a winter being spent on one of the Antarctic bases, thus aspirant fids were affectionately referred to as "fidlets" until the required winter had been endured. This was to produce a social quandary however as air travel became more prevalent. Access by plane was not only much quicker, it avoided waiting until the pack ice had dispersed for ships to get through. Consequently scientists who didn't need the winter experience, started to fly in for "summer jollies" (summer visits) which meant they technically remained "fidlets" - though many find that hard to swallow and ungraciously assume the full honour!

Now, my two years were up and I checked my empty cupboards for the last time. It was time to go, but I thought enviously of the incoming new boys, the fidlets, those who were yet to experience life on this survey base. I thought enviously of new friends, last years fidlets, who would be staying on for a second winter after I had departed. I thought of Johnny Carter and Geoff Smith who had volunteered for an unprecedented third year. There had been a shortage of suitably skilled diesel mechanics and industrial electricians and Halley needed both. When I had heard they were staying I had considered offering to do the same, but I had no non-replaceable skill. I would effectively have become a redundant old lag. Either that or the unwelcome "know all" who refused to move over and give others a chance. The tradition, nay the operational system, was that each year the second year fids passed on their acquired skills and knowledge to the incoming fidlets, who in turn would become second year fids bequeathing skills to the next new fidlets. It was an amazingly effective system but there were a few rather significant accumulations of mental drift that buried previous skills... as I had come to discover. Yes, by and large the system worked, and to deprive a new boy of his maturation would have been selfish and arrogant. Apart from all that, my mother would be very upset were I not on the expected ship. It was time to go. Had it really been two years? Two years of Antarctic wasteland. Two years of wonder. Actually two years and twenty one days with only the other base members for company... and all male too. In fact, counting the voyage south and excluding the all too brief sojourns in Montevideo and Port Stanley it was, wow, two years and nearly three months since sailing from Southampton aboard the Royal Research Ship "John Biscoe" with its all male crew. It was definitely time to go!

A lot had happened in those two years I was to learn later. At home I had gained a nephew, I had lost a grandmother, an aunt and a bedroom, my two best mates had got married, the Sinai six day war had happened (scarcely noticed at Halley), and the miniskirt had been invented. Actually it had been invented in every man's mind for decades, perhaps centuries, but now it was reality. The shock would be quite something on docking in Montevideo again where the miniskirt had not only become the national dress but had reached new heights of excitement. Put that atop those olive tanned, sinuous latin legs of the Uruguayan girls and... But all that was in the future and as yet unknown to us. Still... exploring the unknown was our stock in trade!

Yes, most assuredly time to go. I walked down the corridor between the ten identically sized bunk rooms and past my old field equipment office where the logistics for several expeditions, large and small, had been meticulously and laboriously planned. I called in at the washroom to swill the dust and sweat of room cleaning and rucksack packing from my hands. I grasped the large galvanised steel handle of the outer door and smiled wryly as my damp hands registered the cold metal that indicated the near zero temperature of the unheated tunnel beyond. In two years I never learnt to dry my hands thoroughly and many was the time of a deep winter morn that my hands had frozen to that handle! Once in the tunnel the lower temperature was felt fully but in these summer months and with the proximity of heated huts, the tunnel temperature had climbed just above freezing, denuding the place of its winter decorations. Gone were the banks of drifted snow, the beautiful clear icicles and the glistening crystal clusters. Ignoring all the other huts connected by this one subglacial tunnel I headed straight for the main access shaft, for there was one last place to visit.

I'd been through all the huts of the base a couple of times earlier making certain I had missed no one, but now I headed in a different direction with one farewell outstanding. I climbed the wooden ladder of the main shaft (pleasantly free of snow and ice in the summer months) heading up towards the square of blue sky thirty feet above. There was no convenient front door leading onto a veranda or any such nicety. Halley was built on ice; ice composed of falling snow that hardened to névé and finally glacier ice by the metamorphic action of ageing and the compressive weight of new accumulations. And it didn't melt. With temperatures rarely above freezing, and usually well below, the snow just kept on building, layer on layer, month by month, year by year. Added to this, the buildings themselves had initiated the creation of several large drifts that accelerated the snow accumulation. Shortly after the completion of the hut building phase, the naive amongst us began to realise why we had imported bundles of scaffolding and sheets of corrugated iron. The construction of entrance shafts to each of the seven huts began before snow drifts could block the doors. Over the months, these shafts were extended as Halley "sank" and consequently the wooden ladders inside the shafts grew longer and longer. Now, after two years of snow and drift, the climb was about twenty five feet to the snow surface and a further five to the shaft rim. As I climbed I thought of the many winter ascents I had done, when the shaft sported icicles, and drifting snow had piled on every rung and horizontal surface. The ladders regularly iced up and there had been many a "near miss" story to tell over "smoko", the adopted Navy term for a coffee break. I remembered too the big blow that had cared not for the niceties of flag etiquette. The Union flag that flew above the shaft had been tattered to a mere red white and blue arrow overnight.

Descending the outer ladder I recalled the time we had been dilatory in extending the shaft: we had allowed the snow surface to get dangerously close to the upper rim, and one lad had nearly fallen the full depth when he accidentally walked into the shaft top, unseen in a blizzard. Yes, there had been quite a few occasions, on base and off, when things "could have been a lot worse".

I headed away from the hut shafts, not in the direction of the Muskeg tractors and their promised transport to the relief ship, but in the opposite direction, out past the radar and the beasty hut (ionospherics lab) to a place I visited regularly, the dog spans, the summer home of my other Antarctic friends. It was a calm, sunny and relatively warm day of around -5°C and all fifty five huskies were tethered individually to the long wire "spans". A few were standing but most were curled up into fluffy balls, noses well tucked in, for minus five on a bare nose is still chilly.

Fourteen of these beautiful, powerful, loveable beasts had, in various permutations made up my nine dog team and hauled my sledge with its tent and equipment many hundreds of miles, to places I still dream about. How do you say good-bye to such animals. Animals that not only made the journeys possible, but made them enjoyable and less lonely. Animals that in the midst of the harshest weather, gave we "doggymen" confidence and companionship.

I surveyed the spans but several of my old friends were absent. Whiskey, my old lead dog had been retired the year previous but was then redrafted when we were short of leaders. I had already entered negotiations to bring him home to England for a well earned retirement but he had died in harness. Perhaps it was a more fitting end than suffering the heat of the tropics, or indeed of England. Also the paucity of snow and the loss of his four legged comrades would have been hard on the old fellow. The other absentees included, the old men Skye and his brother Stroma, the gentle bitches Chalky and Snowy. I had run with them all, but they had suffered a more cruel and humiliating fate than Whisky - shot on orders from England. No gratitude, no retirement permitted, not even a humane injection, and no vet to administer it: just an army issue revolver, a box of cartridges, and doggyman who was given the evil job. No one dared ask what he felt... either answer would have been distressing. I could visualise the line in the inventory: "Item, husky, surplus to requirement and written off." I had wept with anger and sorrow as the gun shots rang out in the uncannily still polar air.

I now cast my eye over the spans again. How do you say good-bye? I gazed at those wonderful dogs, so full of energy and vitality, yet now so quiet and peaceful. "Good-bye my friends," I called. Nothing moved. I tried again: "Thanks for all the marvellous times together and the amazing places you took me." Nothing, I didn't have any food for them and I didn't have a sledge or harnesses; why should they respond? My eye lifted to the distant invisible icy graves of those discarded friends, and I felt an unexpected sadness. I took a deep breath, put my head back, and with my best attempt at the Husky tongue, I howled. There was silence... I howled again and felt rather stupid... more silence... then one dog, I don't know which, put back his head and howled also. There was a pause, an anticlimax, what had I expected? But then the cry was taken up by another dog, then another and another. More and more dogs began to hang their plaintive melodies on the still air until every single wonderful animal was howling. I waved, unable to speak as I walked away, homeward bound, the tears flowing freely down my cheeks, and after forty years, my eyes still moisten when I think and write of that parting.

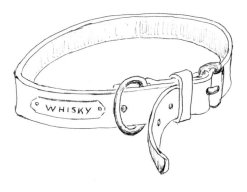

2   Point Touché

"Time to go," called Mike. He had been packed and ready for some time and was probably getting a little impatient. I found it difficult to abandon the place, the scene, the moment, the might-have-been. A few yards from the trampled snow square of our now stowed tent rose our quite splendid ten foot snow cairn. Point Touché we called the place for although there had been no decisive scoring hit against or by our opponent, indeed there had been no face to face duel at all, we had nevertheless acknowledged defeat.   Our adversary, the Shackleton Range, if a lonely group of mountains could be called an adversary, remained inviolate, our every attack parried, until with no aggression served against us, no cutting riposte, we gave in. Point Touché was our furthest south and the closest we would get to that elusive range. We could see several very obvious rock summits or "nunataks" and the domes of some nearer snow hills that formed the eastern extremities of the Shackletons but just how far away they were we could not really tell. Two good days travel perhaps, probably more. Could we have made it? Perhaps but it would have been a close call with little latitude for error, for all we then knew was that we were looking at some mountains that were in the right direction, but the Shackleton Range on the only map then available was shown to be one hundred miles away. The things were looking at were not so distant and the map was obviously incomplete as the "Shacks" clearly extended much further east than anyone had anticipated, however with Antarctica's incredibly clear air and our lack of a range-finder those nunataks could have been be forty, fifty, sixty or even more miles away.

Two other things were certain: we did not have supplies for more than a few days and as we descended from the high plateau, the view of the mountains was starting to deteriorate with loss of altitude. After agonising for a long time we decided to turn back and make sketches from a better view point behind us.

It's amazing how a decision to abort makes one certain the task was possible! At the speed the dogs were running, two days on good surfaces might have put us at the mountains or maybe at a good vantage point. The journey would have been fast as we were on a definite descending series of long steps, each "tread" a couple of miles or so, followed by a short relatively steep descent. Yes, it should have been easy... So why had we abandoned it really?

We could rationalise it but I suspect we were already as far out on a limb as our inexperience and lack of confidence allowed. Two or three days downhill could easily mean four back up and if reaching the mountains were to mean anything we would have to get a bit of rock and some reasonable photographs, which in turn would mean a careful and slow final approach probing for crevasses as we neared the rock - another day, perhaps two. And then what if the weather really turned? After several quite perfect days there were now strong portents in the sky that signalled a significant weather change, a change that would produce heavy cloud cover, and heavy cloud cover produces whiteout. Whiteout can be unnerving as sky and snow merge as one, shadows disappear and the horizon ceases to exist. There is nothing to distinguish a cairn from its background, nor indeed its foreground, nothing to give warning of a deadly crevasse or the large icy nodules that frequently litter vast areas. We certainly did not fancy trying to find our way back in whiteout, but there was also the chance of blizzard. Blizzard has all the disorientating effects of whiteout but adds the debilitating effect of a gale, the struggle for progress, the fight even for balance, the sheer hard work and frostbiting cold. It was a daunting prospect, especially so far from home with no chance of rescue if we got it wrong.

We had calculated our food, had already started our last ten day manfood box and had four days sledging back to the depot. Add those four to an optimistic six days round trip to the Shacks and we would be down to half rations with no margin for lie ups in bad weather. Of course, we could go on half rations, and yes, we would probably have done the whole thing with time to spare, but elated though we were with what we had achieved so far, we lacked the necessary confidence, or stupidity to try for more.

There was another aspect: it was now mid January and there were six hundred miles to sledge back to base before winter set in. Experience did tell us not to rely on twenty miles a day and that both we and the dogs would need a rest part way. Six hundred miles at say sixteen per day plus a bit of rest and it would be early March before we got back. Add a Shackleton push and it could be mid March. At that time of year temperatures would be dropping well below minus 30°C and camping would become more arduous with every task increasingly difficult. Sledging in the "minus teens" and even the early twenties is quite comfortable but below that things get difficult. Boiling water for tea and porridge, and heating the evening stew takes considerably longer and uses more fuel. Packing the tent and stores boxes and lashing the sledge load needs more frequent hand warming stops; the simple need to wear more clothing makes one more cumbersome and operate less efficiently. The knock on effect of all this means that each day's journey is reduced, especially as daylight hours after late February rapidly diminish until total dark returns at the beginning of May.

Confidence, missing or not, the decision to abort was the sensible one, and we had already made that decision. Although making it had clarified our plan of action it had shifted the growing burden of doubt to one of failure and disappointment. I had longed to get to those mountains for reasons of sheer exploration - being the first men ever to visit and hopefully climb them. Mike had in addition a more practical reason for disappointment. I first met Mike Skidmore at the pre-Antarctic briefing weekend in Cambridge in the Autumn of 1966. Little did either of us realise that we were destined to spend many months on field expeditions together but somehow we gravitated and largely spent the weekend together. When we heard we were to be sent to Halley Bay, we were both rather disappointed as the other five bases then in use had mountains and exposed rock close to hand, Halley had neither and seemed a poor destination for us, particularly as I was a mountaineer, Mike a geologist; what would there be to do at Halley? And now, putting the Shackleton Range at our backs, Mike had very good reason for disappointment. He faced the whole winter season with no rock samples or photos to study, no thesis to work on, not even a rough map to plan a campaign for the next year. Mike had real reason for total frustration and every justification for bursting out in anger - but he said not a word. My sledging companion remained his normal easy going, uncomplaining self; a valuable asset when out on a limb and with a long hard drive ahead of us.

"Time to go," repeated Mike. I'd no idea how long my musings and self justifications had taken, but he was right. I turned back to look down the length of the Nansen sledge to those nine beautiful huskies, tensed, alert, waiting my command. Mike holding the harness of Whisky our lead dog, was ready to cast off. My lead dog, I found myself musing: I had become very possessive about "my" dogs though I was only a brief custodian and Mike shared the custody. I swung my skis alongside the sledge runners, grasped the handlebar with my right hand and the skijor loop with my left, and nodded to Mike. "Ok team, home time, Vheet, Vheet away," The dogs lunged forward at the old Inuit call, and Mike simultaneously let go, hooking onto the sledge as it clattered past him. We were going home.

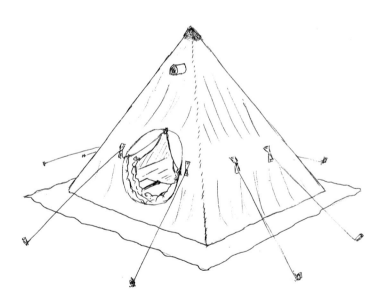

The Camptors 3-man polar tent in orange ventile
Ideal for two men and superior to the cramped & gloomy brown
2-man version by "another" manufacturer

3   Left on the Shelf

Oh ho, here we go
Drink to the land of the ice and snow
Where a scorching day is ten below
Here's to the great white south

One day as I was strolling by the sea
A bearded fellow said these words to me
Young man you look so keen and true
Antarctica's the place for you
Follow me and a polar hero you shall be

Oh no, don't you shun
The glorious land of the midnight sun
Where the beer and whisky freely run
Here's to the great white south

His offer fairly took my breath away
He seemed an honest guy, what could I say
One of the elite, one of the few
Rugged adventure in full view
So I joined his ship bound south for Halley Bay

Oh ho, drink a tot
Here's to Shackleton and to Scott
In whose great footprints we might trot
Here's to the great white south

Now all that seems a very long time ago
All around - uncharted lands I know
This desert of ice I came to see
Am I an explorer? No not me
For I spend my time building huts and shovelling snow

Oh no, we'll not go
To hell with the land of the ice and snow
It's too bloody cold at ten below
You can keep your great white south!

No girls, no sex, no pubs, no beer
Where pinups are the only cheer
And I don't want to be buried here
Down in the great white south!

Halley Bay... could one anticipate or imagine a more inhospitable place to call home? Not the men I hasten to add, but the geographical and physical location. Seventy five and a half degrees south meant Antarctica, some six hundred miles inside the Antarctic Circle but still over a thousand from the South Pole.

Twenty six and half degrees east put Halley south of the Atlantic Ocean on the edge of the Brunt Ice Shelf attached to the main continental ice sheet that, fifty miles to the south and west, commenced its climb to the vast Antarctic plateau, all five million square miles of it. Antarctica is big, very big. Area in square miles doesn't paint a picture in our minds but think of Europe from Portugal to Finland, Scotland to Greece, then add half the USA and that's Antarctica, all but a tiny percent of which is covered deep in ice; ice from a hundred to over four thousand metres thick.   And here, our tiny outpost of civilisation stood in magnificent solitude, totally dependent upon the outside world for every major and minor need, yet almost totally isolated from it. Halley Bay, or Base Z as it was logistically referenced, was first established in 1956 as one of six British scientific stations that would contribute significantly to the findings of the International Geophysical Year of 1957/58. But Halley was unique amongst not only those six but all previous British bases. All those others had been securely built on the solid ground of the Antarctic Peninsula (Graham Land as we then knew it) or one of the adjacent islands; Halley was built on floating ice. True, the ice was around 200 metres thick and felt very solid and was, in fact, in a fair state of equilibrium, for although ice headlands would occasionally break off and float away as icebergs, the loss was amply recompensed by the flow of ice down from the inland ice cap. Vertically there was near equilibrium too since the annual accumulation of surface snow, which never melted, compensated for the erosion by the sea deep underneath. It all seemed reasonably secure and permanent until one realised that a fixed object like an Antarctic base that is being covered by increasing layers of snow and having its foundation depleted was in effect sinking and, because of the flow of the ice sheet, was also getting nearer the coast. We sometimes wondered whether our home would float away or fall out of the bottom! A penguin observation post that was established half a mile from the cliff edge in 1961 was seen about 12 meters down the face of the cliff twelve years later. Extrapolating this rate of descent and advance from inland surface to cliff exposure, the base we were to inhabit (something over 3 miles inland) might have been expected to reach the ice edge around 2040 but some 40 metres below sea level. Considering that Halley 3 that succeeded ours (built 1973) was seen exiting the cliff above the water line in 1993, I guess extrapolations are not to be relied on. Whatever the anticipated date or depth, our ex-home is now certain to have broken out of its icy tomb and sunk. Just one more significant but unseen deposit of man's rubbish in this largely pristine environment.

For us new and temporary residents, musings of sink or swim caused no worry, but it was clear that every few years a new base would have to be built. Building on an ice shelf however did generate one significant problem that affected us all: how to dock and unload a ship of supplies.

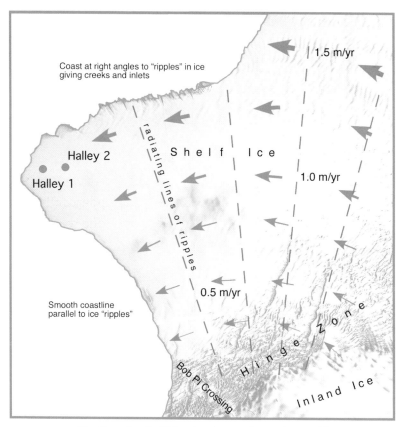

The Brunt Ice Shelf showing the rotation and rate of flow also the creek-forming ice ripples

The location of the Halley bases is approximate, as the satellite photo on which the map is based was taken several years after both bases were lost. Also the coastline had altered because of calving icebergs.

The ice shelf boasted beautiful, flawless, vertical cliffs twenty to twenty five metres high caused by the "calving" of icebergs from its periphery. Unloading up such a cliff is not possible; a weakness must be found in the white rampart and it must be connected to a dock for the ship. Fortunately every winter the sea freezes to sufficient depth to give a solid, if temporary, low and level docking surface on which to unload. This sea ice, known as "fast ice", is attached, frozen fast, to the shelf, but come the summer months it does break away, sometimes during unloading which can prove not just inconvenient but highly dangerous. Even with secure fast ice, the next problem is to find that essential weakness in the ice cliff.

Drifting snow, pushed along by high winter winds, builds up significant snow drifts on the sea ice in the lee of the cliffs. In summer, the sea ice and its snow drifts usually detach to leave the vertiginous white walls rising from ominous blue depths, but where the ice has formed in a significant bay or creek it is often trapped and held for many years. As a result the contained snow drifts grow higher and longer until they form huge wedges of snow reaching from the head of the creek far out into the bay. Simultaneously, this snow degenerates from light fluffy crystals into heavy compacted "névé" that will bear heavy loads. The ramps thus formed from shelf top to sea occasionally make passable highways for tractors, but suitable ramps are rare, for the necessary creeks are themselves rare. Normally, when icebergs calve from an ice shelf, they tend to leave straight cliff lines behind but the Brunt Ice Shelf (on which Halley is built) is quite unusual. Instead of advancing uniformly seawards, it is in fact rotating, anchored as it were in the south west but fed by rapidly flowing ice in the east, and this is the saviour of Halley for the rotation generates great radial cracks which sometimes open as creeks on reaching the coast. Nevertheless even with these ideal circumstances, ramps are rare and rarer still are those that can be ascended by tractors pulling heavy laden cargo sledges, and having adequate sea ice for a ship to dock alongside. Such a ramp is a cherished find, a necessity. Such a ramp existed at Halley Bay and was the reason the first base was built there in 1956.

In 1967 the building of a new base was our prime concern on arrival at this strange flag-waving outpost of British interest. In mid January of that year the Royal Research Ship "John Biscoe" in convoy with the Danish cargo vessel "Perla Dan" chartered from the Jack Laurentsen Line docked alongside the "fast ice". The Danish flag that flew from the headland showed not only the place to dock but also welcomed the Danish visitor. There were four hundred tons of materials and some forty or fifty men to unload. This was the great annual change over of Halley Bay personnel, and many of the existing staff were on the sea ice to meet us. As I gazed out from the security of my ship home, at the ice cliffs rising above the frozen sea, the odd groups of inquisitive penguins, but above all, at that group of heavily bearded and heavily sun-tanned men awaiting our docking and looking very much at ease with their environment, I certainly felt like a fidlet, an Antarctic novice.

Yes, I had visited several bases en route to Halley as "the Biscoe" delivered supplies to Signy Island in the South Orkney group, and Deception Island (before its volcano blew its top and required a rapid evacuation of all personnel). We visited the American base on Anvers Island and that had involved sailing down the west coast of the Antarctic Peninsula. The whole journey was awe inspiring. There had been the wide Bransfield Strait that had then narrowed to the beautiful Gerlache Straits strewn with pack-ice and edged with blue caved glaciers sweeping down from rocky peaks. This in turn narrowed further to the stunningly dramatic Neumayer Channel with its mighty rock summits plunging vertiginously into the blue-black, pond-smooth waters. The air was so clear that Mt Français at 3,000 meters looked half a day's hike. I had even been involved as load bearer and radio operator in assisting Lawrence Willey, a geologist bound for Stonington Island, as he made studies on some of the smaller islands of the South Shetland group. We had then returned to Grytvikken on South Georgia, climbed a nearby peak, wandered amongst the derelict remnants of the old whaling station and paid a respectful visit to Sir Ernest Shackleton's grave. We sailed south once more and had been followed by a wandering albatross, seen massive icebergs - a small one had earlier drifted into our anchorage on King George Island and sat cheekily on our anchor chain. We had pushed through heavy pack ice, been stuck for a few days and seen various seals including the infamously dangerous leopard species. Yes, I had already done more and seen more than any of the yet to be organised tourist cruises, but now, seeing those men at ease on the ice at Halley, I felt very young and very naive.

Sixteen of those men were ready to re-embark after their two year tours of duty, twelve were to stay a further year to be joined by twenty six of we fidlets. Of those twenty six, fourteen would stay a full two years including four of us who, incredible though it then seemed, were to sledge together on the distant Shackleton Range reconnaissance. Indeed, we four would not see another ship for the whole of our duty until our own relief vessel docked in January 1969. Now however, destinations and dreams of dog travel were irrelevant: there was a new base to build and all hands were needed, including those leaving, and those just passing through on their way to other bases. We had just three weeks before the ships sailed and reduced our workforce.

We had barely a month before temperatures would start to drop to the uncomfortable. In two months the long polar night would begin to close in. We had some serious work ahead as there were seven large huts to build...

4   Grillage Village

The first base at Halley Bay, built in the International Geophysical Year of 1956, was a fairly standard heavy timber construction reminiscent of many an alpine chalet. By 1960 this "IGY hut" was deemed to be near the end of its life as Halley expanded and the hut itself "sank" well below the surface. The 1961 huts were built almost above the IGY hut which was kept open for a few more years, but those new huts were less robust and despite the addition of yet another hut in 1964 it was evident that BAS needed to start again with a completely new and independent base on a completely new site. The site chosen was two miles inland from "Halley 1", as the old complex became referenced later by unimaginative staff at head office.   That extra two miles were deemed necessary to safeguard against the new base prematurely calving off as an iceberg and taking a cruise into the southern oceans. The logic was fine provided the ice itself did not destroy the base before it floated away or sank into its watery grave.

Therein lay the problem for the architect: do you make a hut with imperfect insulation that when covered by the snow will sit in a self generating ice grotto? or a well insulated exceptionally strong hut that will withstand the crushing accumulation of ice above?

Halley 1 had tried the former but there seemed to be a limit to the depth at which such a base could be maintained; a limit governed not just by increasingly difficult access but also by ventilation problems and the accretion of water ice that formed around the huts. Halley 2 (1967), the new base we were to construct, would attempt a compromise. It would be stronger than its predecessors but still form its own cavern. Later bases would find new solutions and new problems: Halley 3 (1973) sat inside prepared corrugated steel tunnels, the type of tunnel used as conduits for rivers under motorways or city centres. Halley 4 (1983) went upmarket by building bigger tunnels that housed two storey buildings. Halley 5 (1990) was designed to stay above the crushing ice by being regularly jacked up on ever extending stilts. Halley 6 (2007) is on skis and will be annually dragged out of the inevitably drifting snow to a new location. Suffice it to say, the fact that the numbering system is, at the time of writing, up to mark six, itself suggests the problems of building on an ice shelf have still to be mastered. There are those of us who have dragged cargo sledges out of small snow drifts and know how difficult that is - dragging an entire base clear after a winter's accumulation will be... interesting.

Meantime, back in January '67, I stood surveying a long row of cargo sledges laden with building materials and hoped that someone knew where it all went. Unloading all that timber, steel girders, corrugated iron and sundry other items as well as 750 barrels of paraffin, and a year's supply of food and equipment had been a major undertaking. The paraffin was correctly titled "aviation turbine kerosene" or "Avtur" and was the life blood of the base. In practical terms it was paraffin, but formulated, as the name might suggest, for aircraft engines which, flying at an altitude of ten thousand metres endured the same low temperatures that we were to experience - temperatures at which normal paraffin becomes jellyfied. This Avtur was perfect for the big bulldozer tractors made by International Harvester and for the Rolls Royce generators that provided heat, light and power for the entire base; it was also crucial for fuelling the Primus stoves on our field trips (one never called them "expeditions" until back in the UK). And then there were the crate upon crate of food, box after box of scientific equipment, four yet to be assembled radio masts, two new dog sledges, drum upon drum of electrical cable, gallons of paint, rolls of lino, scores of fluorescent light fittings. The list was endless. Bemused, almost overwhelmed, I continued the unloading; doing as I was told.

The entire cargo was transferred to Halley just in time for within a day or so of depositing the last heavy sledge load the coastal feature of Halley Bay itself ceased to exist. I was billeted aboard the John Biscoe at the time and was awakened one morning by a sudden rough sea. I dressed quickly and dashed on deck to see men and equipment being rescued by the ships' cranes from a chaos of broken sea ice, ice that had for three weeks been our unloading dock. I could not understand how there could have been such sudden damage and such ship movement until someone pointed to the Halley Bay headland. It was a headland no longer but a newly calved iceberg. An iceberg flying a Danish flag. If it survived beyond the Weddell Sea it must have puzzled several south sea mariners. "Why would Denmark claim an iceberg?" they would ask!

A serious critique of that memory, shows a flaw and how a little imagination can become reality in the mind. The truth was that the lost headland capsized and broke into several pieces. Certainly the Danish flag was never seen again and it was the capsize that accounted for the sudden rough sea... but the image of a patriotic little iceberg sailing gallantly up the Skaggerak and then down the Kattegat to an uproarious welcome in København is much more satisfying!

As the John Biscoe retrieved warps and "dead men" (ice anchors), the captain brought her alongside a moderately safe piece of fast ice and all the Halley personnel still on board were quickly disembarked via a rubber chute. As we hurried shorewards to await a tractor the Biscoe and the Perla Dan both put to sea. I thought we had seen the last of them but the

Perla Dan nosed into a narrow bay a few miles up the coast. There was not room to manoeuvre alongside so for the next few days our access was via a rope ladder over the bows - no mean climb and no safety lines. The whole of the headland and the docking was all very exciting and I am increasingly amazed that there was no loss of equipment or indeed of life.

On another occasion the highly dangerous Lansing Snowmobile and its four passengers were also lucky to escape. The Lansing was essentially a Gypsy Moth aircraft engine mounted on four skis with a hint at a cab for driver and passengers. It had been sent to Halley on trial in 1964 but almost instantly declared too dangerous as it needed very smooth surfaces that were rare on the ice shelf. Geoff "Abdul" Smith lovingly resurrected the beast, which was inevitable renamed "Abdul's Flying Carpet", and took it onto the sea ice during the unloading of January 68. A tide crack (a clear water gap in the ice) was seen to be opening between the ship and the shore and the Lansing was on the wrong side of it. The crack was still very narrow, narrow enough to cross, so Abdul claimed. It is difficult to judge widths from a low oblique angle… perhaps Abdul was not aware of this! He opened the throttle and terrified his passengers as he headed for the crack… and there was a crack as they landed somewhat heavily on the safe side. On examination they had lost a rear ski down the now much wider than anticipated gap.

A later "tide crack incident" was more serious and deposited a large vehicle at the bottom of the Weddell Sea. Diesel mechanic Peter Witty was driving one of the big International Harvester tractors across the sea ice to the ship during the 1977 relief. The popular story based on several assumptions is that the sea ice gave way and as the tractor broke through, Peter nonchalantly escaped through the open roof hatch muttering, "Bloody hell, my fags are wet!" The incident was however considerably more dramatic, and had he not been in convoy with Alan Etchells in a Muskeg he would not have survived. The wind had arisen and the spindrift created by it hid a newly opened tide crack. Peter drove his vehicle into the gap but it did not "break through" allowing time for a leisurely escape, it dropped as one might expect five tons of steel to drop. Although in reality the vehicle had no cab (it had previously been removed) and hence no need to negotiate a roof hatch, he nevertheless had serious difficulty escaping as, like Douglas Bader in his plummeting Spitfire, his boot was caught under a control lever. Fathoms down in the Antarctic sea, with broken chunks of ice closing the tide gap way above him, Peter eventually broke free and fought his way to the surface but was then unable to climb out through the unstable chunks of ice. It was Alan who dragged him out but the ice had cracked again and Alan's own vehicle was now stranded on an ice floe. The pair needed help but had only one pair of skis, a necessity in that increasingly dangerous terrain. Knowing that Peter, soaked through and extremely cold, would freeze to death if he awaited rescue, Alan sent him to get help from the ship three miles away. On reaching the ship Peter had to be chipped out of his skis and stood in a warm shower before his armour plating of ice could be removed. A rescue team was able to recover both Alan and his tractor. That both Peter and Alan survived the increasingly hostile conditions is a tribute to Peter's resilience and determination, and Alan's altruistic sacrificial wait.

In 1967 we had excitement but no loss of vehicle or equipment and nor could we complain at the weather. Up to the launch of "SS Halley Headland", we had enjoyed three weeks of sunshine. That is three weeks when, being well below the Antarctic Circle, the sun had circled the horizon, twenty four hours a day, in a permanently blue cloudless sky. These perfect conditions made a potentially difficult build not just considerably easier but great fun. Despite the sub zero temperatures the sun's radiation was so warm that I frequently worked shirtless and in shorts.

It was at the outset that the base earned its name Grillage Village because of the sheets of steel mesh or "grillage" on which every hut was built. This grillage provided a flat platform that allowed the heavy timbers and frames to be moved and erected without carving awkward trenches in the snow surface. The whole design was simple, effective and heavy, and Sir Vivian Fuchs, the Survey's Director, who was on site for much of the time, required twelve hour shifts throughout the entire hut construction phase. The architect, Colin Baldwin, tirelessly and cheerfully advised on every stage, every query.

After the grillage was laid, a heavy transverse beam was rolled approximately into place, a massive steel "portal frame" was then bolted together and slotted into sockets in the beam. Then the entire frame assembly was heaved upright and levered into its correct position. At ten frames per hut and seven huts in all, there was a lot of heaving, grunting and heavy breathing… and much needed pauses to recover. As each new frame was erected, side timbers and purlins were bolted to it and to its predecessor until a twenty two metre long skeleton of a hut stood awaiting its flesh. The "flesh" was prefabricated panels each consisting of two plywood sheets that encased fifty millimetres of insulation sheeting. These panels were nailed in place using six inch nails and short heavy lump hammers. After three weeks of frame erecting and panel nailing I had to loosen my watch strap by two notches!

At two weeks we realised that the six inch nails were running low. A calculation was made and we discovered that, with no losses, no wastage and a certain planned economy we could just complete all seven huts. Nails were not just at a premium, they were irreplaceable. On one occasion I was sitting on a roof, nailing a panel when a glancing blow caused the nail to arc gracefully out of my desperate lunging reach and land in the snow below. I noted its location for later retrieval and took another nail from my bag, but a passing colleague had also seen the incident, picked up the dropped nail and tossed it up to me. There I was on the sloping roof, hammer in one hand, nail in the other and another nail flying towards me. I instinctively popped the first nail in my mouth to catch the second. As the cold registered on my tongue, I ignored the approaching nail and snatched the first from my mouth... and took the skin of my tongue with it, frozen to the nail. I recovered the dropped nail at my colleagues second throw, the recovery of my tongue took much longer.

Even while our hut building team had been lifting, bolting and nailing new hut carcasses, others were working hard to make them serviceable. Of prime concern were the kitchen and the generator shed which were functional in a surprisingly short time and providing food, heat and light in the windowless buildings. Before the outside team could move indoors however, the huts had to be linked by a corrugated iron tunnel. Also short access shafts, that would later be lengthened, had to be constructed at both ends of every hut. Eventually as winter closed in, we were allowed inside and new and varied trades were added to my personal skills portfolio: plumber, painter and decorator, cleaner, cook, radar operator, electrician. It was while engaged in the last of these trades that I earned my polar nickname.

I was working with electrician Paul Wharton as his apprentice when he suggested I install proper lights in the loo instead of the temporary ones wired loosely into the fuse board. Proudly I went off to undertake my first unsupervised job. I anticipated working in the dark so took a torch but was surprised to note that there seemed to be adequate light... Light I should have questioned... light that was issuing from a bulb connected to the fuse board that I thought had been disconnected! Unconcerned I loosened the main feed cable terminals in order to redirect the cable through the correct duct. The bared ends slid out and sprung together and the Rolls Royce generator groaned as the loo was illuminated somewhat more brightly than before. Of course everyone quickly found out the cause of their temporary plummet into darkness and I was known as "Neon" from that time!

The Biscoe and the Perla Dan
        sailed south to Halley Bay,
With summers short they put on quite a pace,
They'd got a team of keen young lads
        with orders from the boss
To brave the ice and build themselves a base

They dropped us on the sea ice
        with four hundred tons of kit,
With tractors and some sledges for the loads,
There were massive beams and RSJs
        and corrugated iron,
Some deep freeze doors and insulation boards.

The snow was quickly levelled
        and some iron grillage laid,
And the mighty portal frames were heaved in place;
We linked them all with timber spars
        on which we nailed the walls,
Then moved on; the building soon became a race.

Seven huts we had to build
        for housing forty men,
With work shops and the base commander's snug,
We'd kitchen, lounge and dining room,
        and generator shed,
And surgery in case we caught a bug.

We knew that 'ere the winter came
    the base would disappear
Beneath the ice, so huts were linked by tunnel;
Windows were a waste of time,
    our front door was quite strange,
Like climbing down an ocean liner's funnel.

The base was thus completed
    and self righteously we said:
"It's the finest," and we thought that this was true,
But the snow came down, the ice welled up,
    the base was crushed between
Which proved to be the end of Halley Two.

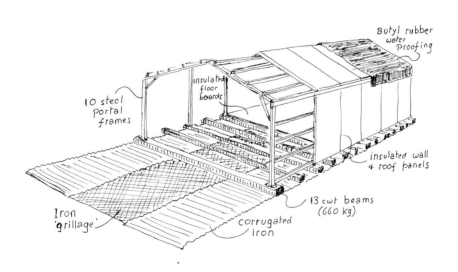

Construction of a Grillage Village hut

5   Shadow of Failure

"*Yerrrr, yerrrr*", another Inuit call and as the remote, unattained Shackleton mountains dropped below the horizon, Whisky swung obediently a fraction to the left taking the team with him. I believe somewhere during Halley history fids learned the commands back to front, as I was later told that Yerrrr actually meant "right" and its opposite *Ouk* meant "left", still, as we taught the dogs the same error it was self cancelling! I called right meaning left and Whisky heard right but understood left. Life was good with the dogs, direct and uncomplicated with no one fussing over correct protocols.

Snow may fall lightly, evenly and quite deeply but provided it has not had time to metamorphose and compact as névé a subsequent high wind can easily remove an entire snow fall and redeposit it as drift in other areas. This leaves behind a smooth glassy surface and I would experience such "glare ice" later, on the high plateau. On that occasion I tried to visit our neighbours in the adjacent tent during a gale but I found myself skating down wind and rapidly losing sight of both tents. An unsettling experience that encouraged us to rig a safety rope between our abodes.

Snow settles reasonably uniformly if there are no obstructions but the sun and wind subsequently play upon it producing variations in its compaction and cohesion. Given sufficient localised cohesion, a good wind can remove much snow but leave harder lumps exposed. The same wind picks up loose surface crystals and churns them together until they lose their feathery points and are filed into miniature bullets.

These ice missiles, hurled along in a gale, blast and scour at the snow lumps, eroding, carving and shaping, with surprisingly beautiful results. The Russians have a word that we have adopted for these snow sculptures: sastrugi.

Many embryonic sastrugi can be passed without notice, but others never fail to attract one's admiration. Some, smooth sided, narrow and arched with blunt snouts nosing the wind look like porpoises, a whole school of them perhaps, arcing from the ice and frozen mid leap. Others, are reminiscent of upturned speed boats, the scalloped angled surfaces like their chined hulls. And usually, nestling in the hollows underneath are clusters of "snowquins", as I liked to call them. Small plate crystals of ice that catch and reflect the sun's rays, each throwing back a different hue dependent on its angle to the sun. Thus in this ostensibly white snowscape one's eye could be captured by tiny glints and flashes of gold and green, pink and purple, cyan and silver.

Today the going was good. There was an absence of sastrugi, which pleasing to the eye as they were, made travel difficult for both dog and man. There was no wind and the sun shone warmly to the extent that despite the minus temperatures, anoraks and overtrousers, even sweaters, were unnecessary. And the dogs were running well, as if they knew they were on the homeward journey - though had they understood the meaning of "six hundred miles to go", they may not have been so enthusiastic!

Indeed the day should have passed in pure pleasure but there was a shadow on my enjoyment. I could justify our actions as much as I liked... but we had failed. The objective of the whole expedition, to reconnoitre a safe overland route to the Shackleton Range had not been achieved. Those last missing miles had nullified all the work and effort, not just of Mike Skidmore and myself (for we were merely the final spearhead) but the whole team.

Even then it was too easy to think of the team as being just the two dog teams left exploring these southern limits, but the field team alone was much bigger (and I wasn't even considering the expectations and support of the folks back on base, nor indeed the boss, Sir Vivian Fuchs, and his team in England). A lot of people had been involved in this exploration and in the final call, I had let them down.

I couldn't really shift the responsibility to Mike for I knew, that although our polar experience was very similar, he looked to me as the mountaineer and doggyman to direct decisions of field safety and sensible practice.

Alan "Dad" Etchells (he was a few years older than the rest of us), the chief tractor mechanic and driver whose Muskeg tractors had got us to a position of final attack, would be disappointed but very phlegmatic, he would cheerfully ask how we had got on, with no hint of criticism. I could expect a similar response from Chris Sykes the other tractor driver and mechanic (he would take over as base commander the following year). Milne "Sam" Samuel, the surveyor in our team who had made the first dog sledge attempt to reach the Shackletons, had, for me, always seemed very private and introspective and I had no idea what he would think, and nor would I ever find out, for along with the other members of our team, Dave Brooke (geologist), Colin Wornham (meteorologist turned doggyman and my mentor) and Alan Johnston (surveyor) he would be back in the UK before our dog teams returned to base.

One person's response I did not consider and never queried was that of Tony Baker (carpenter/builder). What a golden opportunity I had missed in that first winter before the reconnaissance was launched. Tony was a happy guy with a cherubic grin and cheery comment for everyone; always willing to help in any circumstance. I knew he had been to Halley before but regrettably assumed he had spent his time building. Somewhat unusual for a fid he was always clean shaven and lacked the tanned, rather worn countenance that I associated with doggymen. I was to be a doggyman so had gravitated towards the gaunt and bearded. It was some years later that I discovered that Tony along with Sam Samuel was the most experienced dog driver on base, but being somewhat self effacing he never said a word. What could I have learned had we talked?

In mid September '64 Tony and Sam had set out with a strong field party to survey the Heimfrontfjella, a mountain range 250 miles east of Halley but requiring a 50 mile detour to the safest known crossing from shelf to inland ice. Tony, with his sledge companion Dai Wild (who tragically was killed in a crevasse the following year) had then traversed the full length of the 100 mile range working with geologists and surveyors.

In the November, Sam and others returned to Halley to catch the supply ship home leaving Tony, Dai, Lewis Juckes and Simon Russell in the mountains. In April '65 they returned to base but during their 205 days in the field they had suffered many extremes of conditions: temperatures below minus fifty, very deep soft snow, sticky surfaces, half rations and lack of stove paraffin. They had also dog sledged many hundreds of miles in that one season.

I never met most of the Heimfrontfjella team as they had left Halley before or as I arrived on base but Tony and Sam were back for another tour. Sam was obviously a dog man: he was in charge of the field equipment store, he went out sledging and he was on the onerous dog feeding rota, and, in his quiet, light hearted way he provided much good advice.

Colin Wornham had taught me driving and the camp routine; but Tony was there too, untapped. Perhaps the death of his one time, long time sledging companion was still too painful to talk of dogs and men, but his knowledge of what was feasible in extreme conditions would have been invaluable. Perhaps we would not have turned back so soon from the

Shacks! I did have a good teacher however in Colin for during his reconnaissance to the Theron Mountains (the same season that I arrived at Halley) he had had his fair share of unpleasantly low temperatures and hard driving in difficult snow. Some years after his return to England he became a professional mountain guide, and knowing his care and attention to detail, his clients would have been in very safe hands.

Muskeg tractors had accompanied us for many hundreds of miles on the outward reconnaissance to the Shackletons and had established food and fuel depots for our return but they could not stay out all season as the tractors and sledges were needed for unloading the relief ship due in January. Also, several of the recce team were to sail for home on that ship. When the Muskegs turned back to base two dog teams were left in the field to continue the push to the Shackletons, the "Mobsters" driven by Nick Mathys (general assistant) and John "Golly" Gallsworthy (carpenter) and the "Hairybreeks" run by, Mike and me. All involved had put in a major effort to get Mike and me to the jump off point for the final push that seemed at that time to have come to nought.

Although Mike saw the situation at Pt Touché and was involved in the decision to turn back, I knew he must be feeling let down. My geologist companion had not once touched rock. What would they all really think of me? Many years later I met Colin and spoke about my feelings of failure... he wondered what I was blathering about! Nevertheless, now on that return journey and for many years after I had feelings of guilt as I justified what I suspected was a lack of guts. Lack of guts? or was it simply lack of experience? As our... my "Hairybreeks", trotted over the smooth, encouraging surface, I realised that my dog driving experience amounted to very little in real terms and perhaps it had been my very first run, a training run from Halley, that had unduly sewn the seeds of my caution.

6   Sea Ice

It was early "spring", if such a season exists on permanent ice, but the sun had returned after its one hundred day escape to northern climes. Its arrival had been greeted with enthusiasm by everyone on base even though its first appearance on the 10th August was short lived since sunrise and sunset were almost coincidental due north of Halley. For the next ten weeks or so, the risings and the settings would swing round the horizon eastward and westward respectively until they met due south giving twenty four hours of continuous daylight. So would our southern summer with its one hundred days of sun circling above the horizon balance our winter of one hundred days of darkness. But in mid August 1967, day light was still limited as, trying to hide my excitement, I nonchalantly accompanied Colin Wornham, my dog driving tutor, out towards the dog spans. We dragged behind us a newly assembled Nansen dog sledge loaded with all the necessary kit. This comprised emergency food box, cooking gear and tent, navigational instruments, radio... plus nine new dog harnesses made of one inch wide cotton lampwick. This was replaced later by tubular nylon tape that bunched into slippery rope and proved unpleasant for the dogs. We were kitted in the warmest clothing then available to us, long johns, army issue trousers, ventile overtrousers, woollen lumberjack shirt, sweater, kapok anorak with long flap to keep the bum warm and ventile sledging anorak with its deep hood trimmed with wolverine fur. We were told that wolverine was chosen because it had two lengths of hair. The fur certainly worked well as the short dense hair gave a good warm seal round the face while the longer more sparse hairs protected the eyes from wind blown snow but allowed one to see through. Under those hoods we wore woollen balaclavas - mine lengthened to protect the neck as I suspect the stock issue were designed for neckless hulks! Our feet were encased in two pairs of socks, felt bootees and canvas *mukluks* with inch thick felt insoles, designed we were told for the Korean war of the early nineteen fifties. As they were anything but waterproof we felt sorry for the troops operating in the wet, but for us their breathability was a distinct advantage. On our hands were firstly a pair of silk fingered gloves, then woollen fingered gloves (army issue) after that we wore thin felt mittens, thick felt mittens and finally leather gauntlet mittens... and we were still aware of the cold for the temperature was around minus forty. Later, I remembered my old granny's advice about cooling off in hot weather "hold your wrists under the cold tap", she would say, and it worked. It occurred to me that if such a simple operation could be so effective, the wrists must be very vulnerable to temperature. I therefore removed the feet of a pair of long socks, cut out thumb holes in the ankles and wore the legs as long fingerless gloves. These would wrinkle down heavily, Norah Batty style, and provide a thick woollen layer over the vulnerable veins and arteries. With this modification I was able to discard the army gloves and the thin felt mitts and earned greater warmth, comfort and utility.

As I considered our clothing and other gear, Colin attached a brand new rope trace to the front of the sledge. He then drove two aluminium stakes into the snow, one at the forward end of the trace, the other at the back of the sledge, and sledge and trace were clipped to them. This was designed to prevent the dogs from running before time or clanning together in a tangled knot. Initially all went well. In turn each dog of the Hairybreeks team was unclipped from his private place on the spans, helped into his harness and led over to the sledge where he was reattached to his personal short branch off the main trace. There are several ways of arranging a team of dogs but we had opted for the centre trace system it being, so we were advised, easier to control the dogs. I needed all the help I could get so didn't raise a single comment. The dogs were in pairs, along the length of the main centre trace with the lead dog alone at the front. After a long winter of inactivity, the huskies were inevitably excited. I could empathise totally. I tried to hide my excitement by doing as I was told and saying little, but the dogs had the opposite approach, dancing and straining, yelping and barking. Whisky, lead man, was the first one to be clipped on, then came the only bitch Chalky, a flighty temptress, with the carefree, happy, Shem beside her. He was a young dog, Whisky's son, on his first ever run. Perhaps putting those two on early was a mistake Handsome Wensen, named (but misspelled) after the river Wensum in Norfolk, and white with a symmetrical triangle of black on his face, was with his brother Esk (another river) the next to be clipped on. This definitely was a mistake! I was later to learn not to trust the sly, somewhat bad tempered Esk, who proved capable of provoking others into aggression, nor to really trust Wensen who seemed equally short tempered. These siblings were followed by another couple of brothers, two more youngsters: Changi and Luqa. Finally the old stalwarts, yet more brothers, Skye of the crumpled ear (results of a fight) and Stroma also scarred from several early altercations. It was as these last two were being clipped on that excitement at the head of the team boiled over. An alloy stake pushed into soft snow has not even a nodding acquaintance with security and despite Whisky being king dog and with no need to prove it, an impatient growl by one of the rearward dogs made Wensen and Esk respond as one. Their backward lunge at the assumed "aggressor", probably quickly joined by Shem, pulled Whisky, Chalky and the stake into the contest and I was witnessing my first nine dog fight. It was not just awesome, it was frightening, but it was also very worrying. A snarling, blood letting bundle of some four hundred kilograms of fighting dog is a fearful prospect, especially when it dawns on the onlooker that there will be no stopping before serious injury or death occurs. The problem was that no dog could submit to a superior one and back away. These dogs were tied together and the more they struggled, the tighter they were locked in. In futility Colin and I dived for the *thumpers* and circling the animals we let fly with these inhumane short lengths of rope at any bit of dog we could reach. The only creature to back out of the fray as a result of our beatings was Colin himself when one of my wilder strokes hit him squarely on the head.

I am embarrassed to admit that I did use the thumper occasionally at other times but I believe that in that first experience, I began to realise that this traditional fids method of dog control was both cruel and ineffective. I am also embarrassed to say that when I later witnessed a dog being severely beaten by two irate men, I did not have the courage to intervene.

Colin was out of the fray but the fray continued. "Never pull dogs apart in a fight," Colin had said, "If you do it's likely you'll get one dog and a bit of another in its jaws!" But what could I do, thumping didn't work, yelling didn't work, and the tangled harnesses prevented pulling the dogs apart. I decided that the only thing to do was unclip the beasts one at a time and then ease each released animal out of the fight. The problem was that all the harness clips seemed to be deep within the fight.

I aimed at one dog's clip and pushed my hand into the *melée* only to feel a set of jaws lock on. They punctured my new leather mitt and its felt inners plus the woollen and silk gloves and finally the palm of my hand. "No good," I thought as I felt warm blood run down to my fingers, but strangely the offending dog, Changi, seemed to sense that something was amiss; this was not husky blood it was, perhaps, less pleasant! Whatever the thoughts in young Changi's doggy mind, he stopped fighting and I was able to release him and pull him clear. After that it seemed relatively easy to get at each dog and lead him away until only a few were left on the trace and the fight was reduced to a snarling match, and finally peace once more on the blood spattered snow.

Colin and I retired for a rest and an examination of Colin's head.

A much needed mug of tea seemed to revive him and he was keen to start again. With a reduced amount of daylight left and with much greater care, we eventually managed to harness up all nine Hairybreeks. Now I was to learn how to actually drive a dog team. An understanding and pitying assistant, whom I guessed had suffered a similar experience at some time in the past, wandered out to help. He held Whisky out front while Colin and I donned skis, adjusted hats, gloves and goggles and attached ourselves to the sledge - Colin with casual aplomb, me with grim determination. Then we were away. The dogs scarcely needed the call to run as our friend released Whisky, but Colin gave it anyway: "*vheet, vheet*", my first word of a new language.

Fortunately the snow surface was reasonably smooth so that although I had no skiing experience, I didn't suffer too many falls, perhaps the support of the sledge was a significant factor. The main problem was that minor changes in the surface or my weight distribution caused the skis to drift apart or together. The worst was when the outer ski crossed the inner and locked inside the sledge runners. That was a spectacular collapse that perhaps alleviated the previous tensions we had both felt.

We clattered, swooshed and creaked away from base, for even on good snow, sledges are surprisingly noisy. So noisy I began to wonder how Whisky could possibly hear Colin's commands. A quick thought demonstrated the problem: at the back of the sledge, rattling occasionally was a bicycle wheel with its simple cycle mileometer for recording distance run. On either side and slightly ahead came Colin and me with our skis, mine more noisy than Colin's. Then there was the sledge, made of ash spars lashed together with codline and rawhide to allow it to flex - and creak like a man o' war - and sporting hard tufnel lined runners that hit every bump with a bang. Beyond the sledge of course, the dogs, with jangling traces, nine sets of running paws and much hard breathing and panting. And where was Whisky in all this noise? With a four metre sledge and each pair of dogs running in their own two metre gap, Whisky was fourteen metres out ahead of us. I began to understand why the commands had to be so crystal clear, so dissimilar. Indistinct shouts could lead to major confusion, and perhaps be dangerous in crevassed country.

We were some two miles from the coast, those great cliffs of ice that formed the sudden and awe inspiring limit of the ice shelf but from inland or rather "inice", neither we nor the dogs could see them. All we could see at this stage was a shallow depression that marked the descent to the sea ice of the Halley Bay, the topological coastal feature as opposed to the huts we were leaving behind. With so little yet to see, small wonder that Whisky kept wandering off course. And so it was that my dog driving thesaurus expanded: "auk, auk" and Whisky obediently swung right, "yerrrr, yerrrr" and he swung back left. It was fascinating for it seemed that a single call advised our lead dog on the direction we were about to turn, the second call initiated a five degree change. I learned much later that it was unwise to try more than thirty degrees at one manoeuvre else the inside dogs would break ranks to take a short cut which encouraged the outer dogs to try the same. Unfortunately they would be tripped by the centre trace and chaos could reign. I also learned later that the five degree rule was totally unreliable - more a figment of imagination or driver intent; one just kept shouting for a turn until one got the required result.

At the head of the wide snow ramp that led gently down to the sea ice, I learned the fourth and only other command "aaah". It meant stop: a command that every dog knew and never needed repeating!

The spellings of the dog commands are my own interpretation for I never read them in any formal training document (I don't think there was one!) but the spelling didn't matter as we weren't in the habit of writing to the dogs. The pronunciations however differed slightly from driver to driver and no doubt we all thought we had the correct one. Some stayed stolidly English and called "weet" or a superior "hweat", some adopted a French "huit", others tried pseudo Scandinavian with "veet" or "vheet", I even heard "hooeeet", it didn't really matter as the dissimilarities in our various version were easily cancelled by the powerful similarity that the dogs heard amongst the sledge clatter. I suspect though that any Eskimo would have laughed his seal skin boots off had he heard us!

Colin had said we would run down to the bay to look at the sea ice and then, if all was secure, we would skirt round the remnants of the northern headland that had been abbreviated during the ship unloading, sledge along beneath the coastal ice cliffs for two or three miles and then climb back to the shelf via another snow ramp in a narrow bay known as Mobster Creek. The day was heavily overcast and the light adequate but not good. This coupled with the silence and the ghostly blue white of the cliffs lent an eerie feel to the whole place, but uppermost in my mind was Neville Mann.

Atop the headland we were to circumnavigate was a small memorial to Neville who had sledged this very route four years previously. Neither he nor any of his team of four dogs had been seen again. I tried to convince myself that Neville must have been sledging later in the season when the sea ice would be breaking out, for a search party found open water where his proposed route lay, but I knew my pretence was invalid, he had been on an early season training run just like us. I surveyed the view from the cliff foot to the horizon and saw nothing but frozen solid sea ice; I felt no wind that might blow ice away from the coast but the thought of emulating Neville's awful fate would not leave me.

On that first training trip we sledged beneath wonderful fissured cliffs of pure ice, rising twenty five metres or more from the sea ice. We passed an iceberg fast in the frozen sea. We heard, smelt and then saw an enormous emperor penguin rookery - some 10,000 birds I was told. I think we even walked amongst the birds but all I could think of was getting back up to safe ice. Seventeen months later I was driving a three ton tractor hauling three tons of kerosene over the same sea ice, much reduced in thickness and only a few hundred metres wide! On one journey a seal popped its head out of one of the shallow melt water pools through which I had just driven. In August '67 I would have been terrified; in January '69 I simply observed, "if a seal can come up, a tractor can go down," and driving round the pool on all future occasions, carried on ferrying supplies from the ship docked at the ice edge.

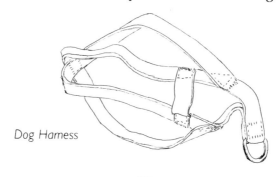

Dog Harness

7   Cairns

"How far now?" Mike asked from the depths of his sleeping bag. It was a conversation piece rather than a query as he knew the answer as well as I. I also knew he wasn't talking about the whole journey back to base for we had scarcely started yet. No, Mike was referring to the depot at flag 13/117, the starting point of our advanced Shackleton reconnaissance, the furthest point reached by the tractors before their return to base, the point that effectively signified that from there on Nick and Golly, Mike and myself plus our two dog teams were on our own.

Every major new route from Halley was given a number and the planned new tractor traverse to the Shackletons was the thirteenth to date. Sequentially numbered flags were planted every two miles, thus flag 13/117 was 234 miles along route 13, which itself commenced at the end of the 200 mile route number 12 that had been pioneered the previous year. Route 12 ran due south from the Brunt Ice Shelf to the newly surveyed Theron Mountains, named after the ship MV Theron that had taken the Trans Antarctic party to its starting point some distance to the west, and some years before. Add to the combined lengths of routes 12 and 13 the 50 miles from Halley across the shelf ice to the start of route 12 and it began to feel a long way home, especially as we had been heading that way for a week now and had covered barely 100 miles.

Mike knew the distance to 13/117 but I guessed his real meaning. On the outward journey we had made a couple of forays onto the glacier only to be repulsed and these repulses had created large dog legs in our final route. It would take an extra day, maybe two, to follow the circuitous line of cairns back to the depot. A short cut was very tempting.

"About twenty four miles as the penguin waddles," I said as I transferred the dividers from route to scale on our almost blank chart. The only marks on the paper being lines of latitude and longitude and the route details I had plotted. "We could do that distance in a day, but we'd better be accurate with the navigation," I added. We both knew the penalty for inaccuracy. If we missed the depot, we would be lost with no reference points.

Mike agreed and reluctantly extricating an arm from his obviously warm bed, stirred the meal that was hotting up on the primus. It was also time for the scheduled evening radio link to the other sledge.

I switched on the battery powered "Squadcall" and as every night, was grateful that we didn't have to pedal a generator like our predecessors who had had to make do with ex-war department "119"s or worse, its predecessor the "68 set" whose batteries had to be heated over the primus to extract even a modest output.

We were effectively testing these new Squadcall radios but unfortunately no one explained adequately how to set them up! We had never heard of "di-pole aerials" so when the radio operator said, "line them up with Halley," we thought it meant point the line of the aerial at the receiving station. Now di-poles should be laid at right angles to the direction of transmission so we rarely got through to Halley which was now some 500 miles away! Fortunately our two sledge teams were much closer to each other and there seemed to be sufficient power in the Squadcall radios to overcome our ignorance.

"Sledge Wog, sledge Wog... this is sledge Ake, sledge Ake... are you receiving? over." In those pre-paranoia days when "political correctness" merely meant a hoped for integrity in politicians, and gollywogs were merely children's dolls, it was perhaps reasonable that a sledge driven in part by Golly Gallsworthy should have a call sign of Wog. I had been, dare I say, more imaginative or romantic, even geopolitically correct. We were travelling in that sector of the Antarctic pie that used to be labelled "Norwegian Territory" when Britain, Australia, France and New Zealand also laid claim to various segments. Possibly because the Americans and Russians and others had ignored these claims and established a significant number of research bases wherever they wanted, the Antarctic Treaty was signed in 1959 and came into force two years later. Although it did not nullify the various national claims, it put them in abeyance for thirty years, for its terms effectively made Antarctica an international continent, owned by none, accessible to all. Nevertheless I had a soft spot for all those old Norwegian explorers and had even started to learn Norwegian, but that was possibly because I had met a very attractive Norwegian girl a couple of years before! Even so, the naming of the territory as Dronning Maud Land in honour of the Queen (Dronning) of Norway was itself romantically patriotic in the tradition of all who claim land that isn't theirs!

If I'm travelling through Dronning Maud's land, I had reasoned, I should have a suitably Norwegian call sign: thus "Ake" pronounced "arker" meaning simply "sledge"!

"Sledge Wog, this is sledge Ake," I called again, "come in please."

Nick must have switched on simultaneously as we got an immediate response: "Ake, this is Wog, you're loud and clear." Initial reports and pleasantries were exchanged and I mentioned our idea of the short cut. They agreed it would be a good idea.

"Pity you're not still at 13/117," I said, "we could have done with a good big cairn to home in on."

"I think you'll be all right," Nick assured us. "You should see Golly's cairn well enough!" and he signed off. Had there been a touch of secretive humour in his voice?

Cairns were the navigational life savers of dog expeditions for it was all too easy to go astray on a totally featureless plateau. The system was simple: travel for two miles or so, place an easily visible marker of some sort, take a bearing to the previous marker, note the bearing and the distance shown on the cyclometer in the journey log and you could then retrace your route.

Tractor parties could carry large wooden stakes that sported numbered flags, but although dog teams carried several mini versions, especially for intricate route finding in crevassed territory, they could not handle the weight or bulk of large flags, and thus relied on snow cairns. We carried a shovel and a saw so their construction was simple. Each sledge duo probably adopted their preferred method and Mike and I developed ours. In fact, cairn design, construction and allocation to specific needs became intriguingly cross-curricular, linking utility with architecture and artistic licence.

Where distances were small or there was no change of direction we would cut snow blocks in about forty centimetre cubes and simply stack five or six of them. Where a greater distance had been run, sometimes more than the recommended two miles, or where there was a significant change of direction, a larger cairn was deemed desirable. After some initial unstable constructions our standard major cairn was built of about nine snow blocks, each sawn roughly thirty by sixty centimetres. After clearing an access channel to the blocks, they were loosened with the shovel at about thirty centimetre depth and then manhandled into a foundation column of four or six paired blocks with the rest stacked singly on top. These were actually quicker to build than the "quicky" shovel cairns that didn't utilise a saw, and did keep collapsing.

Soon we enlarged our tower cairns by building a paired block column on top of a larger three block wide base. Occasionally a special effort was made: "Cathedral Cairn" attempted to emulate Salisbury Cathedral with a four metre high tapering spire buttressed on the two leeward sides - though in retrospect we should have called it Chesterfield Cairn because of its noticeable twist.

"Should be good and visible" we mused, "and could last a long time." It was certainly visible at four or five miles. Whether it would be of use other than on our return trip we could not then know.

In sunny weather standard cairns could usually be seen at a mile and often two as they either glistened brightly with the sun on them or stood out as dark alien blobs with the sun behind.   However, in the overcast conditions that created whiteout, cairns could become invisible at five metres or less. To counteract this we usually carried black bunting material with which to "dress" cairns. There was also a regular supply of brown cardboard that could be torn into sheets and tied onto cairns. This supply came from the large dog food boxes of "Nutrican" bars that were emptied every five days. All this we hoped would give us a fighting chance of finding our cairns again but in whiteout it was even difficult to maintain your distance vision.

Spotting a marker on or near the horizon means that not only do your eyes have to be focused on infinity, but you also have to be looking out horizontally. It was quite amazing the number of times that a cairn would suddenly snap into plain view, apparently in the sky, until you realised you had actually been focussed intently on the ground just ahead of the dogs. If bunting or cardboard were not available we did have one other weapon in our anti whiteout armoury: cocoa!

Ever since the days of Scott and Shackleton it has been assumed that explorers love cocoa... lots of cocoa... cocoa by the bucket full. We didn't! Tastes since the early nineteen hundreds have wimpyfied as modern man has become accustomed to drinking chocolate with its abundance of milk and sugar. Whatever the reason there was a serious mismatch between our cocoa needs and the supplies in our food box. Cocoa powder sprinkled on snow cairns makes them visible over great distances.

•   •   •

The morning after the radio sked with sledge Wog, we set out with high expectations. There had been no new snow for three weeks and being blessed with a cloudless, windless and warm day (-10°C), we were making good progress. I was happily encouraging the dogs by singing them a "travelling song", an on the spot doggy adaptation of "This train's bound for glory". Twenty miles south of 13/117 we homed in on an old cairn built by Colin Wornham and me on an earlier attempt to approach the mountains. Cartographically joining the two routes lent each greater accuracy, the cairn was also a good departure point for our intended short cut to 13/117.

Mike swept the horizon with the binoculars and pointed due north. "One of our cairns," he observed.

"It can't be," I answered, "our route was well to the east. Must be a sastrugi catching the sunlight."

"Sun's in the wrong direction," said Mike, "anyway, it's dark coloured."

"Shadow then?"

"Too dark"

"Perhaps you're right," I conceded, "Perhaps it is one of our cairns..." but it didn't make sense. I pictured our outward route in my mind. From 13/117 it ran due east then swung south and passed our current position still well to the east.

"If that's a cairn," I said at last, "we're seriously off route, and the one we're at is not where I thought it was. The only cairn north of here is… good grief… pass me the noccies?"

Magnified ten times there was no doubt: I was definitely looking at a cairn, not just a reconnaissance cairn thrown up in ten minutes but a serious cairn. "How far to the depot?" I asked, for reassurance.

"Twenty miles."

"I just don't believe it! No wonder Nick said we'd be ok!"

We homed in on the amazing construction and half a day later were impressed. It was a veritable castle at eight feet square and ten feet high with a further six foot normal tower cairn built on top, and the entire side that faced us was sprinkled with cocoa - two ration boxes worth. The lovely touch however was the small christmas tree stuck right on the top. True it wasn't Christmas, it was mid January, but nor was the tree genuine, it was a cardboard cut-out in classic shape complete with plant pot, and coloured with green and red felt marker pens. A leftover from Christmas celebrations on the outward journey.

Nick and Golly had waited at flag 13/117 for news of the outcome of our push south. It was a bleak spot with nothing to see except the featureless snowfield in every direction, but more frustrating, there was nothing really to do. To pass the time, as well as to provide us with a good beacon, Golly had started building… Then on learning of our commenced return, he completed his massive structure and then set off north with Nick to undertake their own piece of the exploration leaving the castle to guide us unaided. It had done its job well but the cocoa, being chocolate brown, had absorbed the sun's modest heat and caused severe erosion!

Mike and I spent three days camped beside the castle while we variously washed (our first in two months!), "chomped goodies" (dined well), and checked, recorded and marked the main depot for future expeditions. That depot, left for we knew not who, contained amongst many other things 2,700 cigarettes and 3 lb. of pipe tobacco, and neither of us smoked!

Meantime, Mike had been repairing the cocoa inflicted damage to Golly's Castle by erecting a block wall against the eroded one. Like our own Cathedral Cairn and even that at Point Touché we hoped it would be visible and useful the following season but whether anyone would ever see it again was open to question. Would anyone ever pass this way again?

Route flag and distant "Shacks"

8   Doctors and Soap

In my journal I have a page listing all the Halley personnel during my stay. Added to those names are their various trades plus nick names, earned or imported. I do have feelings of guilt concerning one good friend from college days who followed me to Halley a couple of years later, arriving just as I was preparing to leave. For some forgotten and certainly undeserving reason, the man had been given a rather unsavoury nickname at college. On seeing this totally unexpected apparition arrive on base I was heard to exclaim: "My God, it's ..." I refrain from committing the sin a second time but unfortunately, that college name resided at Halley another two years!

My journal list includes "John 'Doc' Brotherhood, doctor, dentist, physiologist and nuisance". This is rather unfair and was, even then written tongue in cheek. Polar regions are extremely healthy places to live since the very low temperatures and very dry air discourage the incubation of bugs; or perhaps the total isolation was the main cause. For Doc John, this meant he had plenty of time for his physiological studies, the main thrust of which seemed to be determining how much energy it takes to work in polar conditions - while a doctor sits and watches.

To measure such energy consumption he needed to know how much air we were consuming which in turn meant measuring the flow and volume of the air we were breathing. One might be repairing sledges, feeding dogs, constructing bunk rooms, building access shafts; any of a score of awkward jobs around base, when John would arrive on the scene with his technician Mike Burgin. He was always polite and asked if he might... and Mike would then strap a large perspex box to one's back and stuff a breathing tube in one's mouth. It was like a wearing a 1920s Himalayan oxygen set.

"Just carry on with the job and breath normally," John would say in encouraging tones. Normal? The box restricted movement, especially on strenuous work, and the breathing tube or its air flow meter frequently iced up making breathing either difficult or impossible. Thus the suffix "nuisance" in my journal but I was later to thank Doc John for his dedication and concern.

Colin Wornham and I, with the Hairybreeks, along with Dave Brooke and Mike Skidmore and the Mobsters, had just completed the 1967 early season reconnaissance of the dangerous, crevasse ridden crossing of the hinge zone between Halley and the mainland ice. We were awaiting the tractors to commence the traverse to the Theron Mountains at the start of the Shackleton reconnaissance when I broke a tooth. I radioed base for advice which in simple terms said it would be foolish to start a four month expedition with a damaged tooth. A Skidoo, was despatched from base and Colin and I set out to meet it.

Twenty four hours later I was in Doc Bro's dentist's chair - he had a book in his hand and was studying it feverishly. He admitted that his one week of dental training didn't really equip him to effect a proper repair so he elected to extract. An hour or so and many expletives later we stopped for a coffee break. By lunch time my jaw ached, my neck ached, my shoulders ached and John's arm no doubt ached but I was able to resume the field reconnaissance with no tooth problem at all. Ten years later the last broken remnant of that tooth ejected itself!

● ● ●

Back in the field I remained healthy throughout the Shacks reconnaissance but my sledge mate, Mike Skidmore, did have problems and it was then my turn to render the medical assistance.

With five hundred miles still to go on the homeward run from our furthest south, Mike complained of sore gums. I had read a little about the privations and illnesses of old time sailors and I remembered that sore gums were an early symptom of scurvy. Scurvy should not be a problem for modern travellers, I mused, especially not for us as it is catered for in our supplies. The manfood boxes that we used on all expeditions were singularly and inevitably lacking in fresh fruit and greens so an essential extra was included: a small bottle of ascorbic acid tablets - vitamin C - to be taken daily.

"Sounds like scurvy," I voiced jokingly, "but it can't be," I reassured as I noted Mike's concern, "we take the ascorbic acid and..." Mike grabbed the bottle and swallowed a handful of pills admitting that he hadn't bothered taking them for a long time! His gums were restored to normal in a few days but there grew a second discomfort, that may have been related and was belated. Walking and then sitting became increasingly painful for Mike. At first I thought he was suffering simple chaffing from his army trousers and my unsympathetic journal indicates my intolerance: It reads: "He was unable to bend to unfasten his skis or to sit down. I offered to do outside man duty in his place so that he could lay down to the inside chores but no other sympathy offered as he seems to have plenty for himself"!

Two days later Mike announced that there was blood in his stools, which was rather worrying. But he said his sore behind had been a little easier since it had suppurated the previous night. I chastised myself: it was time to open the medical kit. No wonder the poor man was in pain, his whole coccygeal region was swollen - in short, he totally lacked a builders cleavage. My journal continues: "I performed a minor bathing and squeezing operation. Not much of either was necessary as the sore turned out to be a rather ripe boil which readily discharged a tremendous amount of matter. After a cleaning operation on his posterior I prepared a tasty evening stew!"

In general, humans stayed very healthy but the huskies needed care and maintenance,

Some of the newer dogs born at Halley suffered from, entropion, the result, we believed, of a little too much inbreeding. In entropion the eyelids turn slightly inwards causing the eyelash to brush on the eyeball - painfully irritating which inevitably causes the eye to suppurate and to water constantly. Doc John became expert in treating the disease which involved removing a sliver of eyelid and stitching it back together so the lash turned out.

The surgery for Doc was straight forward but the anaesthetics needed some experimentation. Extrapolating from the human dosage he calculated for the weight of a husky, but not knowing whether the husky physiognomy would respond similarly to humans, he decided on a somewhat smaller dose to start with, adding more as needed. The sight of the first poor (or lucky) dog so treated had every one laughing as it slowly succumbed to the anaesthetic. The first dose had no effect. The second made him tipsy. The third finally put him under but not before a stage of total drunkenness. Two uncontrolled legs on a human drunk is problematic, four uncontrolled legs is hilarious.

In the field we could undertake no such dramatic veterinary work but the dogs were still susceptible to minor injury and a regular duty was to check their welfare and attend their needs. These great beasts were not just work animals, they were well loved, and more prosaically pragmatic, they were our means of getting home. Lose a dog or two to injury and things start to look serious. Fights on expedition could be disastrous if dogs were seriously hurt, indeed on one trip a couple of years earlier a dog had had to be put down when it suffered severe foot lacerations in a fight.

We lacked the experience to appreciate that fights in working teams were rare. In fact I was told much later that allowing dogs to run free at camps kept them happy, it was the perpetual tethering that made them fractious and jumpy. Such advice was too late for us. Although we did try it to a limited extent occasionally, we were always worried that we might lose a few animals which would condemn us to manhauling a too heavy sledge over a daunting distance.

There were the stories of men being unable to catch loose dogs but these always involved dogs that slipped their collar or harness, not those that were given a little temporary freedom.

Dog injuries were not common but running repairs were occasionally needed. For a few days on those first homeward legs from the Shackletons, I had been concerned about Stroma. He had started to limp and on examination I discovered that his toe nails had grown overlong and one in particular was rubbing the adjacent toe causing it to bleed; it no doubt also caused pain by bending the toes upwards every time the poor dog put his foot down as his weight was on his pads not his nails. The remedy was easy with a pair of clippers and Stroma seemed to enjoy the special attention. Indeed he enjoyed it so much he grew his nails again in record time and demanded a second pedicure when I serviced all the other dogs during a respite in the Theron Mountains.

Stroma however had a second problem shared by Esk then Skye, and examination of the others showed the problem imminent there too. As a result, there was some important tailoring to be undertaken on arrival at the 13/117 depot.

We had been unable to dress every dog in lampwick before departure and my forecast about nylon harnesses was proving correct. The tubing was indeed bunching into rope shape, but worse, because it was a slippery material, it was rubbing back and forth with every slight change of pull. The poor animals were being rubbed raw. There was little I could do with our limited resources on the run but back at depot 13/117 there was a good supply of genuine lampwick that allowed me to sew several new harnesses, and after a good "lie up" at that depot, the dogs' sores had healed.

Another problem concerned new snow that could ball up between a dog's toes and if not cleared might force them apart, which itself was painful, but if it packed in hard it could split the skin and cause bleeding. Changi who had particularly hairy toes, suffered from this more than the other dogs but fortunately we had several route flags spare which were cut up and sewn to make a couple of pairs of bootees. Although they would inevitably fall off after a few miles Changi seemed very happy... almost proud.

With the dogs sorted, it was time to wash - a very rare and almost sacred event on expedition - so sacred it was often omitted even by those on trips of several months. Washing was a serious business as an all-over wash in polar temperatures is not to be taken casually.

Even back on base a good wash was not a simple affair. On a frozen continent, all domestic water has to be melted from the native snow and kept warm to prevent refreezing. It's amazing how many large heavy blocks of compact snow are required to produce one decent shower. The rule at Halley was: if you want a shower then you fill the melt tanks, which really meant you only ever had a shower when it was your fortnightly duty to fill the tanks.

In the summer months, tank filling could be quite pleasant exercise but in a winter blizzard it was a serious adventure.

Halley headland
before it broke
away

Perla Dan moored
at sea ice

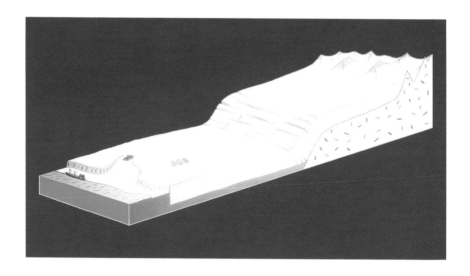

Diagram of floating shelf ice and ramp from sea ice, plus crevassed Hinge Zone

Skeleton of a hut destined to become the lounge

Halley 2 huts completed (Feb 1967)

Halley 2 for ever beneath the snow (Jan 1969)

Shem

Four Hairybreeks and two drivers

Me with lead dog Whisky

Skye

Luqa with Mike

The Mobsters in a
miraged ice basin

Hairybreeks
having safely
crossed the Bob Pi

Nansen dog sledge with 10 day load and survey equipment

1/12 scale Nansen beautifully made by John Gallsworthy

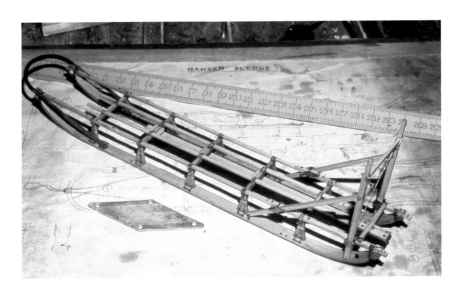

Colin Wornham beside
a big crevasse bridge.
We did not test it.

Paul Coslett dropping a bridge

"Drum Chasm" in the Bob Pi Crossing

One the dog teams did not find

Full outdoor winter gear was needed plus a saw and shovel carried up the ever extending entry shafts. At the top one could be met by a full gale of wind-driven ice particles, but even in mild winds a temperature of minus forty plus could freeze exposed flesh in a minute or so.

Digging out the snow blocks was much the same as extracting blocks for cairn building but as the huts did not keep moving to a new site (as when cairning), the block quarry became quite extensive necessitating an ever increasing carry.

The summer time problem was different: young dogs were frequently allowed to wander free and seemed to home in on the shelter of the quarry for their latrine. One had to be selective in choosing the next block extraction point.

In the loft of each of our two sleeping huts, above the ablutions blocks, were two large stainless steel tanks with electric immersion heaters. Above these tanks, circular holes had been cut in the hut roofs and large fuel drums, suitably topped and tailed and cleaned, inserted to create snow chutes. Like the access shafts to the huts, these chutes grew longer and longer as the seasons progressed. Once the huts were fully buried, dropping the blocks down the chutes was not too difficult but initially we had use a ladder and then negotiate the very slippery butyl rubber roof covering. There was many a slip twixt ladder and lip.

These thoughts were in my mind at 13/117 as I sought out several large pans, a couple of primus stoves and prepared to melt my bowl of water. Although we had sledged in shirt sleeves on several days, stripping off to the natural in sub zero temperatures and then adding water, no matter how hot, is no joke in the open polar air. I looked at my field ablutions shelter: a spare tent with a rubber ground sheet. Even the old base had been better than this I thought, but then changed my mind.

Washing at the old base, the 1961 hut (now entitled Halley 1) had been suffered once and once only. During the building of "our" base (Halley 2), several of us had been billeted at the old base, partly to help keep that base operational until a full transfer could be effected but perhaps more importantly for social reasons as a handful of fids in their second year, were needed, to maintain the old place and its programmes. To isolate them from the new base was deemed bad psychology by our base commander, Ricky Chinn; he was right of course, but it made life that bit more difficult. Showering was the least of the problems.

Early Halley huts, once covered by snow and if not too heavily insulated, created their own snow caves and sat inside quite snug, sheltered from the harsh winds and winter temperatures. Unfortunately the generator at the old base was quite sickly and had stopped producing adequate power for the heating system, no heat escaped from the roof and the cave grew smaller and smaller until its top started to press on the roof of the hut.

One only has to see any valley or mountain ridge carved by ice to appreciate its implacable weight and force. Halley 1 was not just very cold, it was being crushed, with us inside. I recall putting a ladder up to the loft to extract some personal kit. I left it up overnight and could not remove it the next day, it was jammed against a lowering rafter. A day later there was a noticeable if slight bend in the ladder. A week later it had buckled to almost thirty degrees. It was under these cold and crushing conditions that I took my shower.

A five gallon oil drum was suspended from the ceiling. A tap complete with sprinkler had been attached. It remained only to fill the drum with hot water, an awkward and tedious task carrying water pan by pan from the coal fired stove in the kitchen and then reaching up to empty into the shower drum. Few people bothered to fill the drum but this led to a different problem. The drum being opaque, one couldn't tell how much water had been used. The fear was to be left fully soaped with no rinsing water. There was however a benefit as an efficient wash might reward one with a longer than anticipated rinse. But regardless of one's efficiency, the air was cold and the floor was cold, very cold. Showering was a necessity, not a pleasure.

A week or two after this self inflicted initiation rite and with little regret we quit the old base - the ladder sported a right angle bend.

• • •

With some trepidation I crawled into the wash tent at 13/117 and with even more trepidation stripped off completely. Kneeling on the cold rubber floor I wetted, soaped and dried, in turn, face, neck, each limb, then body and finally tackled hair (by now quite long), all the time hoping there was enough water left to rinse. It is said that the body becomes self cleaning after a few weeks but whether or not that is true or just an old hippy excuse I don't know, I do know that that all over wash in fifteen degrees of frost and seventy nine degrees of latitude felt very good, especially when I donned clean underwear and shirt - the first in two months!

The Old Base Shower

9   Lie Up

Rest days or enforced "lie-ups" were a perfect opportunity and excellent excuse for "goody chomping", especially when camped beside an imaginatively stocked depot with appetising food. The goody chomping at depot 13/117 was indeed quality dining. I made an oven out of an empty biscuit tin, placed it over the primus stove and cooked a joint of pork that had thoughtfully if optimistically been sent out by the Halley cook. That, plus a selection of inevitably frozen greens, dried onions, dehydrated potato mash and stuffing, all suitably reconstituted and hotted up, made a splendid first course. Desert was pineapple. Manfood boxes were very basic but depots, I reflected, were generously stocked. Add to that the cheese and biscuits followed by Drambuie and we contended for the "best Antarctic restaurant" award.

A few days later however this culinary achievement was totally outclassed when we joined Golly and Nick at depot 13/90. The menu card (yes we wrote one!) read:

Pineapple juice
Mushroom soup
Fillet of Herring in Horseradish Sauce
Roast Pork Cutlets scattered with fried Kidneys
Runner Beans with minted New Potatoes
Christmas Pudding with Rum Butter and Brandy Sauce
Coffee
Cake, shortbread, nuts, biscuits
Drambuie & Cherry Heering

It's hard living on camp rations!

Later we realised we had the potential for a literally flamboyant desert even when out of range of a food depot. Powdered egg, powdered milk, flour and medicinal brandy produced exquisite Crêpe Suzette.

• • •

Quenching cravings for good food was not the only purpose of a rest stop. "Lie ups" were frequently forced upon us by awaiting the arrival of other teams or by inclement weather. Lie ups ranged from the sublime to the frustrating, and I was to learn much later, the frightening. Despite not moving, we always got up, even though much of a lie up, as the name implies, would be spent laid upon our beds. "Getting up" seemed important and anyway there were always the dogs to attend and minor jobs to be done.

On pure resting lie ups we would potter in peaceful bliss, sunbathing if there were no wind, reading, attending to clothing repairs, checking the tent. We would regularly find small abrasion holes in the tent fabric and these would be mended with pre-glued ventile patches lest a high wind found the weakness and ripped us open to the elements. I used to make the repairs fun by cutting the patches into various unpatchlike shapes - hearts, clubs, diamonds, spades, pentagons, hexagons. Our tent became quite... pretty?

The Nansen sledge would also be checked over - but despite all its hard battering it never needed any maintenance. We would spend time writing our journals, plotting the route on the largely blank paper called our map, calculating supplies, estimating journeys, and just dreaming. On such rest days in the quiet, sun-bright, solitude of the polar ice, life was good. What more could one ask for.

Snug, warm, relaxed and alone
I lie contented with my little world;
My orange, pyramidal world,
My simple world
Whose length and breadth is but an arm span;
Whose every content known, named and numbered.
I have everything I want.
I am my own master
And master of this world.
Here is security, comfort
But seemingly misplaced or lost,
Lost amidst five million square miles of ice.
A harsh, inhospitable white desert;
Bleak
Blank
Barren.

But I am happy and at peace
I have every thing I want;
My eyes close....
I commence my transcendence
To the other world of day dreams
"You have everything."
Says a small contented voice within my mind.

The orange fabric of my world dissolves:
Translucence
Transparence,
A window.
I gaze through this dream window
I gaze through time and space
Another place
No ice, no snow, no solitude
("Everything you want?" asks the voice)

Here are people, many people
Laughing, talking, drinking
Everyone happy in each other's company,
Yet all are strangers to me.
Save one...
("Everything you want?" the voice wavers)

Save one...
One who for me spells perfection;
Across the room I see her silhouette
Her softly waving hair
Her exquisite form.
I sense her beauty
Her excitement....
("Everything?"... quavers the voice
Nothing - the voice and I collapse in despair)

I look with longing
And she turns
And starts with surprise
Astonished at my proximity;
Laughs with joy.
Oh what joy is to be mine
That tinkling scintillating laughter,
Those twinkling stars in her eyes
A paradise of merriment, of beauty, of femininity
A whirlpool of delight
Drawing me inexorably closer
Closer
Closer...

But two paces betwixt us,
But two seconds before we meet,
E're we kiss....

But they are paces of an infinite league
Seconds of an infinite hour
All this in one imagined window pane
One window of pain.

The ice cracks with my broken joy,
The clouds cry crystallised, crocodile tears
That, caught in the guffaws of mocking wind
Splash and splatter upon the window
Deforming, distorting, contorting
That once so lovely image.

The wind shrieks with buffeting laughter
And gathering handfuls of snow crystals
Hurls them with derision
At my opaque flapping window
That accursed orange window
Of my now so empty world.

Fortunately such descents into the depression of lost opportunities and nostalgia were not the norm. Lost opportunities? I had to accept the she dumped me not the reverse! The only thing I had dumped was a small field depot near the Shacks just a week ago.

On a number of lie ups, I invented and developed the idea of a new board game that was going to make me money. It was called, inevitably, "Antarctic Reconnaissance" and was a cross between Monopoly and Snakes and Ladders. The lads politely showed great interest and back on base I even drew out the game board and made the various "chance" and "skill" cards. Obstacles of "chance" were, would you guess, crevasses, whiteout, soft snow, blizzard, leaking paraffin... what else! Skills included, surprise surprise, good dog control, the ability to recognise hidden crevasses, accurate navigation, good sledge preparation... Many years later I discovered a game about downhill skiing that worked on a similar principle - it wasn't popular even though downhill skiing is. What chance a game about sledging in some unknown part of the world! It remains an undeveloped memento in my loft.

The lie ups forced upon us by bad weather on the Shacks return trip were more frustrating and, according to my journal, were considerably more frequent than my memory of prolonged sunshine allows. We knew the sledging season was drawing to a close and we were still many miles from home. It could only get colder, darker and more arduous. We wanted to keep moving but when you can't see the next flag as you drive past it, it is time to stop. A strong side wind easily blows one off course and gradual, cumulative errors could prove fatal when heading for a known crevasse field.

Except for the lack of sunbathing, the days of these bad weather lie ups were passed in similar manner to the sunny rest days but there was always an underlying tension: When would we get going again? What would the surface be like? Would there be an accumulation of "deep soft" making it hard for us all, dog and man, or would the wind have scoured away the loose stuff to leave good fast running? Or would we be pinned down by "deep whiteout"?

Many alpine skiers have experienced whiteout and all find it difficult to handle, but *deep* whiteout (as I term it), when the cloud envelops one as fog, is especially difficult. I recall recently stopping on an Italian ski slope in deep whiteout conditions to wonder at a strange orange object that was ascending the slope towards me through the mist. It looked like a snow canon but snow canons do not trundle up hill unattended. It was only when I accepted that it *was* a canon that I realised that it was in fact stationery. Although I thought I had stopped, indeed felt to have stopped, I was still sliding gently downhill on a collision course. That is deep whiteout but on a blank polar icecap with no snow canons or other distinctive feature it is far worse. The fog of course reduces visibility, and many a hill walker or sailor will know of the difficulty of judging the distance even of things that can be discerned through the fog, but true whiteout obliterates all detail - sastrugi, cairns, crevasses, all are invisible. If there are no contrasting features (there are none on the Antarctic plateau) it is the nearest thing a sighted person can get to being blind in broad daylight.

In crevassed terrain, all whiteout is dangerous and forces a lie up for better conditions. On flagged routes over safe terrain, lie ups are not necessary, provided the cloud has not descended to fog conditions, as the only things to take one by surprise are sastrugi and that the next flag is always above or below where you think it should be. Nevertheless whiteout, that random scatter of uniform light rays that give neither shape, shadow nor colour, always confuses the senses.

A bright heavy blanket enshrouds our world
A flat world of unbroken white
Featureless
Uninspired
A new canvass awaiting it's Renoir
A blank manuscript hoping for Brahms
A clean page before its Joyce
A dead thing pleading life
Pleading new horizons

For there are no horizons
They have fled this all white world
As though required elsewhere
To separate laughing deck-chaired sands
And shrilling bare legged sea
From blue-white gull gliding summer skies,

That little children might look beyond
Their castles in the sand
(Castles in the air?)
And exclaim "Look Daddy
"A Ship out there on the horizon!"

We have no horizon
And no ship defines it.
All around in silent conflict
Cloud and ice vie for superiority.
Sun's rays, that once gave form and colour
Now are scattered and contorted,
Reflected and distorted,
Diffusing confusing,
Until some sympathetic wind
Or frolicsome breeze
Drives off the cloying cloud.
Then once again
Sun shines, shadows cast,
Form is restored, distance focuses,
Horizon reorders ice an sky

But now, cloud ensnared
One thing only defines our world
Whiteout.

It was in whiteout that I was involved in my first crevasse incident. During my early months at Halley two lads had sledged out from the base on a dog training journey to see the penguin rookery on the sea ice, but on the way back, in gathering dusk and whiteout (more a blueout in the gloom!), they had encountered a narrow unseen crevasse, barely a couple of miles from home. Seven dogs, a sledge and two men crossed safely, one dog fell in but was held on his harness and quickly extricated but the ninth member of the team a young bitch called, Moo on her first ever run, fell in and dropped out of her harness. In cross section the crevasse was a slight S shape and it tapered with depth. The drivers did not have the means with them to extricate Moo so returned to base for assistance.

Colin Wornham, Jo Porter (GA), Big Al and I set out armed with ropes, wire electron ladders (as used by potholers), stakes, pulleys, crampons and anything else we thought useful. It was going to be a difficult job, we could not see Moo who was beyond the first bend, but we could occasionally hear her whimpering. Someone was going to have to descend the crevasse and it fell to Colin as main doggyman.

He started down the electron ladder but as the crevasse narrowed, progress became very awkward and constricted. After sixty feet or so he could squeeze no further and still could not get a good view of poor Moo, some ten to fifteen feet below. Colin was slim but Jo was even slimmer and was a mountain rescue expert so he took over the attempt. He managed several more feet by letting his feet dangle and descending hand over hand, safely belayed by a rope from above. It was now impossible to understand what Jo was shouting as he could scarcely turn his head, and the ice muffled and distorted his voice. A second safety line was rigged and I followed him down to a half way point in order to relay messages.

It was clear that Moo had fallen further than Jo could possibly reach so a loop of rope was tried but the poor dog was jammed so tightly there was no way of passing the loop round her. It was also getting dark and we could scarcely see what we were doing so returned to base for lights and a long pole with a hook lashed to the end. Jo and I descended again, the lights illuminating the whole crevasse. The pole was passed down and Jo tried to hook Moo's collar, but the tightness of the space prevented him from accurately directing his efforts. He could force the hook down level with Moo's head but it was impossible to engage it under her collar. Moo was tightly wedged on her back, her jaw, legs and shoulders making her collar inaccessible. Jo probed and pushed and tried every possible manoeuvre for a long time but the result was always the same... and then he realised that Moo had made no sound or movement since we had returned, she was very probably dead already, I hoped she was.

On the way back up the ladder the lamps highlighted a large sharp spike of ice pointing upwards and covered in blood with great streaks of blood below it... even had we extracted Moo she would most likely have died from obviously severe injuries.

It was a melancholy group of men who silently returned to base, each no doubt wondering whether the poor dog was indeed dead and if not how long she would suffer. I for one also hoping that if I were destined to fall down a hole and not get out alive, that my death would be mercifully instant.

● ● ●

Thoughts of possible disasters, near misses and might-have-beens can invade one's thoughts in a lie up, especially if pinned down by bad weather and particularly if surrounded by crevasses.

Essential reading!

10   The Slessor Glacier

I crawled into the tent, shuffled off my boots at the door and sat for a few minutes thawing the ice from my beard and moustache.   It was a job that could not be hurried as impatience led to pain. I also had other pain to deal with: the leather mountaineering boots I was field testing were proving excellent in every respect but one, they had given me rather large blisters on my heels. I considered changing to the canvas mukluks but knew them to be too warm for continuous dog driving. I didn't want sweaty feet that could rapidly turn icy once I stopped moving; apart from that, different boots would not cure the blisters.

I removed my socks and examined the damage: the view was not good. I thought I had tried all then known solutions but there they were raw, red patches on my heels and the size of half crowns in old money. It was a process of logical deduction that produced an answer that stood me in painless good stead for not merely the rest of the journey but on all future occasions.

It occurred to me that a) skin is there for a purpose, b) if it has been removed it should be replaced, c) skin does not roll around like a normal strip plaster dressing, so d) stick something over the replaced skin that won't roll or rub.

Pieces of lint cut to size and shape replaced the skin and they were held securely in place all round by generous pieces of wide sticking plaster. Much later, on another journey, I caught the blisters before they burst, which caused me to contemplate the cause of the pain. I realised that the blister itself (which was there to protect the abused area) did not generate the pain, it was the hydraulic action that walking on the blister creates. The blister fluid is forced sideways and tears skin from underlying flesh. That's what hurts I reasoned, and concluded that popping the blister and then stabilising the loose skin with the wide plaster and no dressing would do the trick: it did. It was so successful that I advocated the method to many of my students and many a mountain leader when I later worked in outdoor education.

When feet and other immediate chores had been attended to we considered our situation. We were now approaching the agreed rendezvous with Nick & Golly from where the long circuitous route home would turn west following a one hundred mile dog leg along our outward route via the Theron Mountains, but Nick and Golly had not been wasting their time. Once Mike and I had commenced our return from Point Touché they had set off north to probe a possible direct route back to Halley. Unsupported, there was of course no chance of their actually crossing the high plateau but anything we could learn of the "diretissima" would assist future expeditions. Their journey had been both frustrating and boring. Frustrating in that their dog team, the Mobsters, had turned lethargic; boring in that they suspected and proved that they would simply travel for five days over the very flat plateau, see nothing and then sledge back again, but the boring nature of the route made it perfect for tractors. Although our southward push towards the mountains may have had the potential for glory, their northward effort provided a valuable indication of a practicable route without which even we doggymen might have abandoned all hope of a second attempt on the Shacks. The line they had taken had slowly converged with the established route from Halley to the Theron Mountains and that route was known to be boring - ie. safe. There was also another old safe route probing south where a temporary ionospherics observation post, Coats Station, had been established in 1964. Nick & Golly's northerly route actually overlapped this, ending some fifty miles to its east, but as the whole region seemed so uniform, the direct route from Halley to our present position seemed eminently feasible, and by-passing the Therons would reduce the distance by that hundred mile dog leg. What's more, with no crevassing on the plateau, the journey could be run without dogs, giving a pure tractor traverse.

Though I loved working with my dogs, the concept of a tractor train that would be unconstrained by the limited daily mileage of dogs was an exciting prospect. I was anxious to transmit our news and idea to Halley and to London but atmospheric conditions or more probably our misdirected radio aerials did not yet allow this.

The rendezvous for our two teams was not merely the westerly turning point nor simply a convenient opportunity to reduce the stock of chompable goodies at the depot, it was effectively the head of the Slessor Glacier.

Yes... the Slessor Glacier... the bane of our expedition and the reason we were reconnoitring north as well as south. The reason our homeward journey was six hundred miles and not three hundred and fifty!

Full of optimism our full field team had left Halley the previous October with the intentions of not only completing the geological survey of the Theron Mountains, 250 miles south of Halley, that had been started the previous year, but of establishing a new route from the Therons due south again to the Shackleton Range a hundred miles or so beyond.

Heading out to the Therons on the first stage of the reconnaissance we had two Muskeg tractors that were originally designed for traversing the muskeg swamps of Canada, terrain of soft peat and moss, but with their wide tracks were found to be excellent on snow. So good were these vehicles that they were adopted and adapted by ski resorts as *"piste bashers"* to create and groom ski runs. Our Muskegs each hauled three large cargo sledges, the first sledge entirely loaded with fuel drums, the second had food, survey equipment, and general spares and supplies; the third carried a full team of nine dogs in specially built kennels. We thought we were doing them a favour and conserving their energy by not requiring them to run, but in retrospect I suspect they would have been far healthier and happier had they pulled empty Nansen sledges alongside. Much better this than being cooped up in a small kennel all day: a kennel that rose and banged down hard at every bump on the icy surface.

I also suspect it would have been better for the men too to have taken turns running with the dogs instead of being either cooped up in a stuffy cab or freezing outside on a sledge.

One particular day comes to mind, a day of three significant events: Firstly it was my birthday, secondly it was celebrated astronomically with a near total eclipse, and thirdly I nearly died. Muskeg tractors have cramped cab space, sufficient for a driver and two friendly passengers, so at any one time our two vehicles sheltered six men. There were eight of us and it was my turn outside.

The heavy laden convoy trundled on in second gear at a modest walking pace, the best they could manage. I rode a while, walked a while, climbed on the various loads to check security and then decided to check the dogs. There was little standing room on the kennel sledge so I stood on the cross bar of the "A" shaped tow frame and leaned on the nearest kennel that housed Fedu, a fine looking young dog, one of a litter of six males all named after World War II RAF air bases and of which my own Changi and Luqa were brothers. The kennels were open at the top but there was a thin spar of timber across each to deter any attempt at jumping out. The spar across Fedu's kennel was misaligned so I tried to straighten it. It seemed stuck. I pulled a little harder... still stuck, so I gave a good jerk... The spar snapped, and so abrupt was that snap that I lost balance and fell backwards into the triangular hole of the A frame.

One of the modifications that had been made to the cargo sledges was the addition of lashing points, four inch bolts projecting out and down from the rear and front cross members of the sledge. These bolts were some twenty five centimetres apart and the sledge was so laden they were scarcely clearing the snow surface. Fortunately I had fallen with one arm over each limb of the tow bar and was able to hang grimly on. At first the reality didn't hit me; I'd fallen, hadn't hurt myself and I would get up and carry on what I had been doing. But I couldn't move! The slow drag of the snow on my body cancelled all my efforts to pull myself forward onto the A frame. And then I saw the lashing bolts only a few inches from my feet. If I let go, the sledge would hook my boots and then slowly grind over me ripping and crushing, mincing flesh, splintering bone to leave a mangled red pulp in the convoy's wake. And no one would know until I failed to claim my cab seat in an hour's time.

Shouting was useless. Between the steel cocooned driver and me were two high laden sledges and a scarcely silenced six litre diesel engine.

It was a moment for superheros but there wasn't one to hand unless it were me for how I escaped I still don't know. One moment I was being dragged along envisaging an agonising death, the next I was sitting on the A frame. The old comic strip phrase comes to mind: "and with one mighty leap he was free."

Somewhat hysterical with relief I rejoined the others. They asked what was funny. I told them I fell into an A frame, they laughed at my clumsiness but I caught the look on Dad Etchells' face. He knew about the bolts, the zero clearance and the fact he would have known nothing as his tractor train slowly crushed and disembowelled me.

The rest of the journey was uneventful except, and partly because of my near miss, we rearranged the loads and Colin Wornham and I erected a tent on one of the sledges. Now we outside men could travel in relative warmth, comfort and style in our "Pullman" compartment, we and need not wander around risking life and limb. Indeed risk was quickly forgotten in the quickly christened "keg-a-tent" for the comfort of our airbeds far exceeded that of the cramped tractor cabs to the extent Colin and I were reluctant to exchange. We, experimented and soon found we could secure a primus stove to prevent it capsizing and so were able to keep plying our drivers with tea and coffee. The height of achievement came when I managed to cook a meal for all eight of us while on the move. Considering the very basic ingredients (meat bar, curry powder and few herbs and tomato chutney), the basic facilities (primus, pan and spoon) and a rocking bouncing kitchen it proved to be a meal *par excellence*. The undemonstrative Sam Samuel praised it and begged seconds, Chris Sykes (a non-curry man) conceded it was good, others nodded approval and even Dad allowed that I was improving!

"A hundred miles from the Therons to the Shacks... Easy peasy," we thought as we approached the Therons depot site.

The Theron escarpment lay before us, a long and massive wall of vertical rock to the east, another to the west and between, a jumbled chaos of icefalls surrounding other vertiginous cliffs. It was a barrier to further southern progress except for one weakness, the Goldsmith Glacier, a major ice stream that splits the Theron escarpment, a stream of ice that points due south straight at the Shackletons. Here we left Colin and his dog team to assist Alan Johnston finish his Therons survey while we tractored on to the head of the Goldsmith where Nick and his dog driving mentor Sam set off with their team to reconnoitre the next easy-looking stage to the

Shackletons. As the anticipated extra two hundred miles round trip for that phase required more tractor fuel and supplies than we had been able to carry on our Therons journey, Dad, Chris, Mike and I immediately returned to base with the tractors for fresh loads that included Golly who would replace Sam when he went home. On our return to the Therons the local work was finished and the Muskeg party plus Colin and Alan set off in pursuit of the Shackletons bound dog sledge.

We met Sam and Nick at the head of the Goldsmith Glacier. It had looked like the obvious route but problems were foreshadowed by Sam's & Nick's long faces. The Therons had been left behind and an easy fast run enjoyed to the edge of the broad "low lands" that lay between the two mountain ranges but then large crevasses and chaotic ice had been encountered barring their route. That low lying region was the Slessor Glacier, first discovered in its lower reaches by Sir Vivian Fuchs' party on the Commonwealth Trans Antarctic Expedition nine years earlier and named in honour of RAF Marshal Sir John Slessor, chairman of that expedition's committee. Neither "Sir Viv" nor we knew the glacier's extent but we were to discover, and what we discovered was impressive. At 250 miles from its snout on the Filschner Ice Shelf to the safe passage we eventually found round its head, and 100 miles wide at that head, it might not claim Guinness Book of Records status but it was big, very big. But then, what defines a glacier that descends from a five million square mile ice cap? The first crevasse? The first significant slope? Increased ice flow rate?

As yet unaware of the extent of this monster glacier, Sam and Nick had turned east in an attempt to circumnavigate the Slessor's head. Time after time they had tried to find a safe route south only to be repulsed on every occasion and each time the crevassing appeared further north. They had been forced not just east but north east and we had wanted them to go south. Finally a fortnight after the first rejection when they were seventy miles off the hoped for route they decided to return to the Therons to meet the tractors. The task seemed hopeless.

After weighing up all possibilities which really meant "Do we go home or keep going?" we decided to keep trying, and following Sam's and Nick's return tracks, turned due east at right angles to the mountains, now visible to the south. On reaching Sam's and Nick's furthest point we found crevassing straight ahead and for the next fifty miles, like them, the only progress we could make was north east. Another forty miles eastward was then permitted before at last there was an opening south but it was too late. The mountains we were aiming at were now a hundred and fifty miles abeam (as the Snowy Petrel flies) and we still could not go direct. I joined Colin for another recce with the Hairybreeks and the Muskegs followed at a safe distance but when we radioed yet another blind alley, Dad had to call it a day. It was imperative he take the tractors and half the crew back to Halley. The Muskegs were needed for unloading the supply ship, and three of our field team were to sail home.

In reality the crevasses we encountered on those forays into the Slessor might well have been quite normal for an ice plateau, perhaps the Slessor was not as extensive as we thought but without doubt, when Mike & I finally turned west towards those elusive mountains there was a marked descent and an increasing frequency of crevasse fields. I'm sure we did not find the world's largest glacier but it certainly ranks amongst the biggest. More importantly for us, glacier or not, those eight hundred or more square miles of dubiously crevassed ice field made a singular obstacle and were the reason our geologists Mike Skidmore and Dave Brooke took no rock samples home from the Shackletons... not even to decorate a mantelpiece.

It was at flag 13/117 that on the 23rd December 1967 that the tractor party depoted its final payload and departed for Halley having advanced us fifty four miles beyond the great southerly turn. That turn was flag 13/90, one hundred and eighty miles from the Therons, one hundred and fifty from the Shackletons, four hundred and thirty from Halley.

• • •

Flag 13/90 was the return rendezvous and as Mike and I sledged in we discussed how to link a possible direct route from Halley to our current explorations. Nick, on radio, suggested we adopt a version of Amundsen's technique for finding supply depots. At right angles to the line of travel Amundsen planted stakes at easily intervisible distances on each side of the depot. In the top of one set, notches were carved, the others left plain; thus if they missed the depot but found a stake with a notch, they turned right, if no notch they turned left. Very simple and very effective. We could go one better, for a cargo sledge of empty 45 gallon fuel drums had been unloaded at 13/90. After pitching camp, Mike and I loaded our empty dog sledge with four of the large drums with their screw caps removed. We then made an easy round trip to the west, depositing the drums every mile with the cap hole uppermost. Nick and Golly undertook a similar exercise to the east but their drums had caps on and were planted upside down. Thus even if the drums blew over, the cap or its absence would say which way to turn. In the event we never saw these guide drums the following year but due to the amazing accuracy of our navigator, Norris Riley, we homed in direct on 13/90 which we had enlarged as a pyramid of three drums and a tall wooden stake topped with a metal reflector.

Nick, Mike, Golly and I, very heavy in the gut after our lie up and sumptuous blow out at 13/90, agreed that it was time to go. Mike and I had done all we could to the south, Nick and Golly similarly to the north, the homing beacon had been erected, all the depots had been checked and double checked and I had plotted our routes, our depots and the directions of our mountain sightings on the almost blank map. There was nothing left to do other than head for base.

Four days after leaving depot 13/90 we once more saw the Shackleton Range, the Eastern Shacks as we now called them; the domes and nunataks that had been visible from Pt Touché. This was extremely useful as now being able to recognise individual tops we were able to take good intersecting bearings to provide more accurate fixes on the embryonic map. The corrected positions added to my conviction that a direct tractor traverse from Halley to the Shacks was eminently possible. They also resurrected my feelings of guilt and failure when those fixes produced a short fall in our recce of forty mile. Just forty miles. We could have done it, couldn't we?

Nevertheless the sightings seemed a very positive omen and that the same evening we at last managed to contact Halley Bay. We reported our achievements and made our proposition about a direct route next year, asking that permission be obtained from London Office. Full of anticipation we signed off and I began tentative plans for a major expedition the following season.

Many years later when I encountered modern maps of the Shackletons I was able to plot our route and the distance from Pt Touché to that lonely range and discovered our position fixes across the Slessor to have been rather inaccurate. The distance to the nearest rock was not forty miles, it was a twenty eight... just one good day's run down hill.

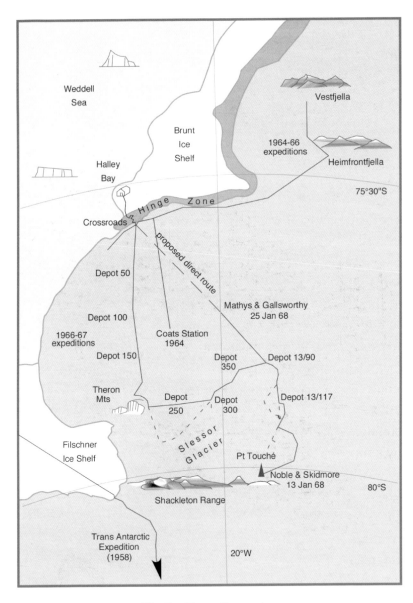

The Shackletons Reconnaissance

Showing the depots, the attempts to cross the Slessor Glacier,
the route finally taken round its head and the the propsosed route
for the following year.

11 A Touch of Frost

For some days as we ran the homeward traverse beside the Slessor Glacier I had become increasingly annoyed by delayed starts every second morning, the mornings when Mike was inside man. The frustration had subsided during a timely and much enjoyed rest in the Therons, and I suppose I hoped we were back on a cooperative schedule, but as we left the mountains behind, things seemed not to have improved. It was my turn as outside man and as such my duty was to prepare the dogs and the sledge for travel while Mike packed the tent innards. Together but in silence, we then packed the tent and when all was ready with various boxes and bags lashed to the sledge, Mike skied across to Whiskey at the head of the team. He extracted the tethering stake, and as I removed the one behind the sledge I called "Up dogs, *vheet, vheet*". Another day's run was underway.

After a mile or so I turned to Mike and striving for the right words and tone of voice, said: "Mike, I have a complaint, can we talk about it?" It was all very civilised. In the back of my mind I had the image of an incident on base when a disagreement had been sorted more physically. There were very few armed forces personnel amongst our mainly civilian team so when a newly promoted sergeant tried to pull rank on a corporal our non-services diesel mechanic planted a non-commissioned fist on the sergeant's nose. It stopped the rank pulling but it did not help the atmosphere on base which remained strained for some time.

On a long field journey with a single tent companion, a

much more restrained addressing of problems was needed. Anyway, such a dynamic approach was also totally unwarranted for my frustration was in reality quite minor.

As outside man I would try to be ultra efficient in preparing for the days run, not merely because I hated time wasting but because it was cold first thing before we had got the blood circulating. Mike on the other hand seemed to be taking things more and more leisurely such that I would be left to stamp about in the cold waiting for him to emerge from the tent. It never occurred to me that my anger was in fact making me work faster which made the apparent delays even longer. On a few occasions, instead of a friendly "Hurry up Mike, it's damn cold out here", I pulled out the side guys of the tent to let him know that I was more than ready to pack it onto the sledge. Inevitably this not only angered Mike, it made his job harder as the tent walls flopped inwards. I had also compounded the problem by working extra fast when undertaking my inside man role so as to be packed and outside before Mike was ready with the dogs; just to show him it could be done. It was in retrospect quite childish on both our parts as Mike admitted to slowing down when I made my obviously critical gestures.

In very controlled tones we each expressed our growing anger, we listened and appreciated the others perspective and the difficulties were amicably resolved. It was ultimately a model of conflict resolution but there had been too much introspection and self righteous frustration beforehand. Fortunately and perhaps surprisingly, that was the only disagreement that Mike and I had on that or any subsequent work we undertook together.

Would that all personnel problems could be so easily handled, but how does one deal with a man who refuses to undertake his allotted work, the work for which he was employed by BAS, when he admits he is only there for a "jolly". Or the guy who "forgets" his dog feeding duty on a particularly harsh winter day and then refuses to get out of his bed when reminded? Or the tractor driver who "forgets" to fill up his petrol tank at the start of his shift. This last omission may not seem particularly sinful but refuelling was a long, tedious and arm aching job, and contriving to shift the responsibility to the next driver was quite unkind.

The Muskeg tractors were equipped with 45 gallon fuel tanks and on long expeditions we generally used about half a tank per driving shift. It was therefore prudent and standard practice to top up with petrol before starting one's drive to avoid running dry on the "second" half tank. It was also less arduous topping up half a tank than a full one. The process was crude but effective. Each tractor pulled a tanker sledge loaded with twelve fuel drums, so rather than unload a drum and roll it to one's own vehicle, one simply stopped alongside another tanker sledge and refuelled direct without unloading. The tedious, arm aching part was pumping the fuel from tanker to tractor using a hand cranked, short swing, rotary pump. As each action transferred only a pint or so, a half tank required around three hundred strokes! "Forgetting" to top up avoided this hard labour but also condemned the next man to six hundred strokes - provided one didn't oneself run dry en route.

On the occasion that I particularly recall, the "forgetfulness" did backfire. I was driving in a tractor convoy when I was flagged down by the disgruntled driver of the lead vehicle who had indeed run out of fuel before his shift ended. The ensuing six hundred strokes was punishment enough and deterred him from a second bout of forgetfulness!

This sort of self centred attitude to life in the Antarctic was not merely annoying, it could be potentially dangerous and on one occasion jeopardised the outcome of a reconnaissance expedition by dog sledge. Avtur fuel for the camping stoves was stored in a jerry can on the sledge and transferred as needed to a smaller tent tin. To avoid carrying too much avtur on the sledge, the jerrycan was itself topped up periodically from the large drums at depots laid by Muskegs. While camping beside an avtur drum depot, I asked my outside man to refill our near empty jerrycan. No avtur: no stove: no tea. Reluctantly he donned outdoor gear and left the tent.

The pumps used for Muskeg refuelling were too heavy and cumbersome to be carried on dog sledges, and as it was obviously too difficult and dangerous to try to pour avtur from drum to jerrycan, we always used a long syphon tube. A light, flexible rubber syphon tube needs constant support and attention, especially on a windy day and I assumed my colleague was providing the necessary attention as he seemed to be absent from the tent a long time. Eventually I was forced outside for more personal needs to find no sign of my tent mate and the syphon tube swinging freely in the wind, draining precious fuel onto the snow. My outside man was snugged up inside a neighbouring tent, chatting and drinking tea, and the fuel loss was considerable. Very little had reached the jerrycan but worse, there was now little left in the main drum. It was only the fact that the other sledge teams had already topped up that we were able to share avtur and complete the reconnaissance. What particularly griped was the total lack of apology or any sign of remorse. It was all the fault of the wind and the syphon tube!

I refrain from naming the various culprits as forty years on I'm sure they would be most embarrassed to read that they had caused so much aggro. I am also quite sure that I too gave my own share of annoyance to others but perhaps the brevity of this chapter indicates that Halley was on the whole very well mannered and civilised. There I learned that "cooperation, consideration and commitment" are crucial for a successful and enjoyable outcome; to the extent that I adopted these three C's as the motto for my outdoor pursuit centre some years later.

12 Cold Comfort

Back along the north side of the Slessor we became aware of a more awkward frustration, certainly more protracted than a few minutes wait for a tent to be packed. This frustration had a name: the Mobsters. Nick's team were the same in number, weight, vintage and experience as ours but they just did not run well. I felt sorry for Nick and Golly for it was obviously a real struggle to keep their team moving; I felt sorry for the dogs as the drivers' frustration would boil over and they would take it out on the team, especially Nuga their lead dog who seemed to have a mind and will of his own. By contrast it was a joy to run with the Hairybreeks. The second team usually has the easier time as there are well defined tracks to follow and the dogs don't, or shouldn't, need directional commands, added to which the sight of another team ahead should tempt them onward without exhausting encouragement. It must have been galling for Nick and Golly to see the contrast between our two teams and we considered using the Hairybreeks as lead team throughout but Nick admitted that this would add to their own frustration. Generally therefore we alternated the lead each day but when the 'Breeks were following we would often leave camp up to an hour later than the Mobsters and still catch them long before the next camp.

The journey was nevertheless most enjoyable and beautiful. White snow against a wedgwood blue sky and nothing to mar its perfection. Gradually the Western Shackleton Range came back into view with two notable summits, Mounts Sheffield and Absalom we believed, clearly visible despite their still being over a hundred miles away. Using binoculars I made sketches in order to check our assumptions back on base, assumptions that subsequently proved correct.

It was about this time that we encountered an initially alarming deposit of a particular kind of hoar frost known as "depth hoar". Glacier ice has a fairly uniform temperature below the surface but at the surface, it is influenced by the air temperature. If the air temperature drops well below that of the ice, then ice in the "warmer" lower layers sublimates (same idea as evaporate but direct from solid to vapour) and redeposits within the colder surface layer. This has two effects, it creates a hard icy crust and leaves the lower crystals seriously weakened. Subsequent snow falls can add layer on layer of firm sound snow, sending the weakened layer deeper. This is "depth hoar". We had met the phenomenon before on many occasions, indeed we had to remove depth hoar every time we built a cairn. The excavated blocks would frequently and easily shear at the depth hoar layer. Occasionally the useable snow was only a thin sheet but more usually it sheared at around twenty five to forty centimetres. If the depth hoar were not scraped off before erecting a cairn the whole structure could collapse. Depth hoar underneath ones feet (or skis) is unnerving.

As we sledged along, gazing at the mountains, encouraging the dogs, we suddenly felt the sledge drop between us and fractionally later we dropped also. It was only a matter of perhaps an inch or two but that first drop was most alarming. The time is milliseconds but the mind and the imagination work in nanoseconds and one has already broken through a big crevasse to the blue void beyond before the reality dispels the fear.

On this day the first depth hoar collapse was quite localised and very sudden and it was some time before we encountered the next drop, but as the day wore on we experienced more collapses that grew in extent and frequency. We were getting quite nonchalant but as we were setting up camp, the whole tent dropped, shaking the stove and rattling the utensils within. The sight was quite amazing. The area of our camp was quite hummocky in polar plateau terms and the depth hoar collapse, that seemed to have originated under our tent, continued as we gazed about in awe. We could see the continuous collapse as a ripple radiating outward in every direction as though a stone had been dropped in a pond. But this pond ripple was not silent, there was a rushing crunching sound that seemed to echo around us. We could see the disturbance climb an undulation and disappear over the top when the sound would die away, only to come again as the ripple visibly rose over the next undulation. It was difficult to put a duration or even a distance to this remarkable event. Memory says half a minute, maybe only ten seconds, perhaps much less but it was impressive.

Our homeward route took us back through the Theron Mountains and it seemed the ideal place for a short holiday. Not only did the dogs need a rest but so did we, especially Nick and Golly. Skiing beside a dog sledge for eight hours a day is serious work but psychologically we also needed a break. We needed a bit of fun and something different to do. Those few days in the Therons were exactly what was needed. We wandered onto a couple of mountain tops, trundled a few boulders (much frowned on nowadays) and made short ice climbs with axe and crampons, all totally relaxing and enjoyable. We even tried the dangerous sport of straight line down hill skiing - no one knew how to turn!

Some years later in Scotland, my bemused ski instructor could not understand how I could run, jump, herring bone, star turn and side step, in fact negotiate virtually any obstacle on skis but fell over as soon as I encountered a down hill slope!

Fondest of all memories of that Therons sojourn however is simply being in the quiet and solitude of the camp in beautiful scenery. Of friends who could be relied on, who gave companionship and conversation when needed but who valued their own solitude and respected that of others. Of dogs, curled up and sleeping after their dinner. Of steam from our own dinner preparations issuing from the vent in the apex of the tent. Of a sky, speaking with crystal blue clarity, punctuated with a few wispy cloud commas. Of a sun low but warm on the face: all quite idyllic.

Too soon the Therons were left behind, the days passed and we climbed once more to the high plateau where temperatures fell. We had enjoyed a few scattered days of -8 or -9°C but generally it had been in the mid teens, quite comfortable, especially in no wind when we found anoraks and overtrousers unnecessary. By late January however the more normal temperature was around minus twenty five and some time in mid February the sun set! This event was only a brief midnight dip below the southern horizon but heavy cloud covers hid the event for several days. We knew however that with only ten weeks or so to total winter darkness, sunsets would get rapidly earlier each day, nights would get longer and temperatures drop further. On the plateau between the Therons and Halley -33°C was recorded and we still had a fortnight of sledging ahead. By this time we were used to the discomfort that low temperatures bring. Most noticeable and first on waking were the twin discomforts of cold feet and ice on the inside of the tent. The alarm would wake us at 6 a.m. and the "inside man", the man with responsibility for all the inside jobs that day, would tentatively reach out of his sleeping bag, prime the primus stove, and snuggle back for a couple of minutes as the burner heated. A well tuned primus would then self ignite and needed only a pump or two to get it roaring. Water, melted from snow the previous night, and now refrozen as solid ice in its pan was then put on for tea. The "outside man" would lay there pretending to sleep and ten minutes would pass before a mug of excessively steamy tea was set beside him on the food box containing ten days' rations (when full), that was always placed between the heads of the two men. Too hot to drink, the wait was almost unbearable for the results were known. The wonderful liquid would seem to fill the arteries, course down the legs and warm the toes and that permitted stolen extra sleep in warmth and comfort. Meantime, the inside man was back at work preparing porridge. One half pint mug of porridge oats to nearly three of water with milk powder a little salt and veritable icebergs of butter - we got through six pounds of butter every ten days both in the porridge and spread thickly on lunch time hard tack biscuits. The amount we ate was quite prodigious but we were burning over 6,000 Calories a day.

Finishing the porridge meant the outside man had to stir and this was unpleasant. The heat of the stove had by now melted the ice on the inner tent such that it ran with the melt water and condensation. Dressing had to be undertaken speedily but carefully to avoid contact with the tent and then came the unpleasant task of untying the still frozen door tapes and pushing through the wet fabric to check and harness the dogs for the day.

Four dogs spent the night on, appropriately, a night trace. This was a thin wire that at camp was clipped to the front of the main trace then pegged out at right angles. Four individual short traces like those used when running were spaced along it and one dog of each pair was transferred to its sleeping quarters. This we hoped would ensure that dogs and men enjoyed a peaceful night but it didn't always work. Esk, who later showed great promise as a lead dog, developed the habit of slipping his harness during the day and refusing to work. When he then slipped his collar at night and I found him nosing the food box I recalled Colin Wornham's tale of a dog named Satan who had done the same thing with dire consequences. At the time Colin was himself a novice doggyman assisting glaciologist Bob Thomas on a survey expedition. Satan was one of Bob's more powerful dogs whose unfortunate antics not only curtailed their journey for lack of dog food but - in Colin's own words:

> "Satan sniffed out the Nutrican which had been transferred to a sledging box, bit through the plywood and tucked into about twenty bars. The next day and for the remainder of the trip, apart from being bloated, sluggish and constantly eating snow, he seemed not to have suffered any major side-effect. But a few days after returning to base he was found dead on the spans, we thought either as a result of extreme dehydration and kidney failure or of a gut constriction. Very sad because he was a powerful and much-liked heavyweight worker."

In hind sight, the dog food supplied did not equate to the dogs' daily needs. The ration we were told was one and a half bars per dog per day. One and a half bars! Had the supplier ever tried cutting a bar in half at plus twenty degrees let alone minus twenty. The only practical solution was to give the beasts one bar one night and two the next. Why the manufacturer didn't supply larger bars I'll never know - perhaps BAS never told them of our needs and usage. Another oddity of the dog food was that each bar was wrapped in greaseproof paper which, again we were told, was part of the diet: roughage it was called! I somehow doubt if it was good for the digestion or the diet but it certainly scoured the system. Perhaps it was twenty sheets of greaseproof paper stuck in the bum that had done for poor Satan.

Esk, was a saint in comparison with Satan and gave us no serious night problem but about the same time young Luqa was showing signs of distress, yapping almost hysterically at night and playing up during the day. I suspected that Esk, always a loner, but who was nightly tethered between Whisky and Chalky with Wensen off to his right, might be feeling crowded; Luqa on the other hand was a very sociable, if slightly insecure animal but his nightly quarters were at the outer end of the night trace. I simply swapped the two and we had no more trouble with either dog.

It was on the plateau that Mike and I also experimented with allowing one, then two dogs to run free for a while at camp but we were always worried about the consequences of a lost animal and soon abandoned the idea. Perhaps the memory of certain cheeky, fluffy bundles wandering freely around base had engendered a little sentiment for even as I re-tethered Stroma I smiled at the recollection. Soon after arriving at Halley, when all the dogs were still at the Old Base, six pot-bellied balls of fluff were transported there from the ship. Someone said they were puppies so they were duly deposited in the pup pen near the big dogs. They didn't like the idea of being penned up so cunningly opened holes in the wire mesh and padded over to the stock of seal meat for a feast. Everyday they escaped and everyday we would tuck one under each arm, pop them back in the pen and repair the new hole. Eventually we admitted defeat and took them up to the new base (Grillage Village) where they could wander freely without fear of attack from an adult dog. There they would troop around in an unruly gang demanding attention from anyone they encountered. Once they were acknowledged they would engagingly drop their head to one side and positively grin until the human object of their focus gave in and petted them, whereupon, they inevitably rolled over waving numerous legs in the air. Unfortunately this freedom and trust backfired when a dog team was driven in from the Old Base. One of the pups, ever inquisitive went to investigate and was savaged to death by one of the team. I never found out, nor understood why some of the dogs, bitches actually, should be so aggressive with puppies.

As I called for Shem to return from his own momentary freedom and clipped him back onto his night trace my last thought of inquisitive pups was a happy one. For their own safety, when the big dog spans were moved to the Village, the pups were securely penned between two huts. Gradually snow accumulated until one drift reached the eaves and lapped up the roof. One morning we watched the pups mountaineer up the drift, scramble up the roof, sit on the ridge and toboggan off the other side to land in a happy heap - free again.

· · ·

"Winds getting up," observed Golly at one rest stop. "Should we camp here?" It was more a statement of preference than a question and it seemed a good idea. The wind was indeed increasing and sinuous lines of spindrift, not more than calf high, swarmed across the desert like a migration of white snakes. There had been a heavy cloud cover all day giving whiteout conditions and several times we thought we had missed a marker flag only to find it either above or below our line of sight. Now, the rising wind had fragmented the clouds giving better visibility but it would not be long before the "snow snakes" coalesced into a deep and wide sea of spindrift that would make flag spotting even harder. Also, the longer we travelled in the brewing gale, the harder it would be to set up camp.

Though high winds inevitably made tent pitching more difficult, the process was in reality extremely easy. If the designer had not himself camped in polar regions then he was very well advised. The tents were made of orange ventile cotton that gave a pleasant living light. Pyramidal in shape they had four stout aluminium poles, one up the inside of each ridge and securely attached thus maintaining the shape. This arrangement not only gave great stability and rigidity, it obviated the need for a vertical centre pole. This aspect earned its Brownie points as soon as one entered the tent for it allowed near standing height in the middle of the tent; height which, when not used for standing, was used for hanging gloves, boots, dog harnesses and any clothing that needed drying.

Suspended from the tent poles and made of tough nylon was the inner tent that provided quite effective insulation and an amazing feeling of security. Each tent section had a wide flap or valance round the base, the inner valance turned inwards and prevented snow working its way onto the rubber ground sheet which lay on top. The outer valance spread outwards and allowed shovelled blocks of snow to be placed on top securing the tent and eliminating draughts. Two guy lines on each side added to the security but mainly pulled out the walls increasing the living space.

The aspect that made for ease of pitching was that the poles did not need assembling nor fitting: everything, apart from the ground sheet was of a piece. The whole tent unit was stored in a long bag and all one had to do was extract it, grab a couple of poles each, pull them out sideways and the tent was pitched. True there was still the valance to be weighted and the side guys to be pegged but that was the outside man's job.

As soon as the tent was standing, the inside man bundled inside, spread the ground sheet, and his colleague then passed in the various necessities. These were quite specific: First off the sledge were two post office bags containing our personal kit. Today, Mike as inside man received these, opened both and took out our sleeping bags and mats - air beds were inflated and covered with a rectangular fleece. Loosely stowed double sleeping bags inside their protective canvas covers were unrolled and allowed to air and loft. A call to me, the outside man, and I stopped pegging out or shovelling and passed in the food box followed by the "U-box" or utility box that contained the paraffin stove, pans and various cooking utensils and repair kits. By the time I had set the night trace, unharnessed and moved the dogs, optimistically laid out the radio aerial, placed a supply of pan size blocks of snow by the door between the inner and outer tent, opened the Nutrican box and fed the dogs, filled the one pint paraffin can from the large jerry on the sledge, rechecked the tent, rechecked the dogs... there was a hot brew waiting, a comfortable bed, and "scradge" was well under way.

Scradge! The fids adopted and totally accepted the word for the main meal of the day. At Halley the cry of "scra-adge" would summon us to excellence on a plate such as roast beef and Yorkshires or lamb casserole. In the field, although we did manage the occasional blow out with quite sumptuous cuisine, the standard main course definitely earned the title "scradge". Batchelors dehydrated meat bar was the main constituent to which was added dried onion flakes... and that was it! Theoretically we were supposed to add a portion of dehydrated potatoes but as there was only one small packet in a ten day food box and that packet barely served a healthy appetite for two men at one sitting, we always reserved the potatoes for the tenth day then ate the lot. The same applied to the breakfast tinned bacon. Not only was the supply quite pitiful, but the end product, the usual scrap of sad flesh floating in fraudulent bulk-adding water, was not worth the effort or mess of cooking each day. That tenth day therefore could be anticipated with some relish - even the limp bacon.

The regular evening meal started with soup. Like the cocoa, we were once again at the mercy of our historic forebears. Scott's team complained at the abundance of tomato soup and the lack of brown soup. Of the ten soups provided in our ten day ration boxes, four were oxtail. This may not sound excessive until one has consumed oxtail for two in every five days for two months or more; indeed it was not unknown for new food boxes at depots to be raided for their tomato, mushroom and chicken soups, condemning the next users to total oxtail. I suspect that rather than oxtail becoming dissatisfying, it was the knowledge of the great variety available coupled with the lack of interest or imagination by the box packing company in England that caused frustration and rebellion - after all the meat bar never changed and we accepted that. In reality however, we did not accept the unchanging meat bar without a fight, we disguised it.

I always carried a small tin labelled "scradge disguise" that contained ten plastic bottles of various herbs and spices. It worked quite well giving us pseudo lamb (with mint), roast turkey (sage mixed with the onion), chilli con carne (cayenne pepper), bolognese (garlic salt) and curry of various grades from "did-you-actually-find-the-curry-powder" to "pass-me-another-chunk-of-ice". The overly flavoursome mint, thyme, sage, curry powder, garlic and marmite was not a success!

Years later, a colleague produced a Batchelors meat bar at a Halley reunion and for the first time I read on the wrapper that Batchelors themselves recommended flavouring the meat bar! I guess the packing company never read the wrapper either. There was one other deficiency in the manfood box, sugar, though *deficiency* is perhaps too strong a term as it depended on the sweetness of one's tooth; even so sugar was regularly supplemented from stocks on base or, like the soup, stolen from unopened field supplies. On the return from a Theron Mountains trip I was camping with Dad Etchells when sugar, or the lack of it, became an issue. Now Dad liked his sugar and always ladled a handful of five or more cubes into his tea; I took only one. Assessing our dwindling supplies one day as he performed his alchemy of transforming thirst quenching, delectable tea into sickly syrup, he announced that supplies of sugar were running short and at present consumption would not last until we reached Halley. "We'll have to ration," he declared, "we'll each reduce by one lump."

The tent had one final good design feature: the tunnel or sleeve entrance. There were no vulnerable triangular flaps, no zips; both inner and outer tents had large circular "portholes" for doorways. These were protected by long "sleeves" that could be tied open on warm calm days (-5°) but would be bunched up and tied with tape in cold or windy conditions. This made a very effective draught proof, non-jamming seal against the weather. Tedious though entry or exit could be in inclement conditions, (untying the two tapes, crawling through the sleeve tunnel and retying the tapes) the simplicity and security were worth the extra effort. But there were occasions when assistance was needed, and that evening as the wind reached gale force on the high plateau was one such occasion.

Perhaps it was the increasing cold that had made the day's start more difficult, perhaps the dogs had needed more cajoling, perhaps I just didn't feel the need to "go". Whatever the reason, that need now came upon me in earnest, but serious preparation was required.

Trousers and underwear were removed, I then donned an extra sweater and my sledging anorak and secured both high around my waist. Next came the loose fitting ventile overtrousers pulled high to cover the bared nether regions, and finally my sheepskin "tent boots". Meantime Mike had untied both tent entrance tapes and was clutching the closed ends of both sleeves; a wicked, rather-you-than-me grin on his face.

"Won't be long," I said.

"I'll time you," he replied, and meant it. "Go."

He let fly the tent sleeves and I dived out into the blizzard.

"Not bad," he said a very short time later, "twenty seconds!"

"And paper work completed," I answered.

We laughed but we also knew that with no shelter and exposed flesh freezing in minutes, one couldn't afford to hang about (as it were!)

> Some men have conquered Mount Everest
> Some men have flown the North Pole
> Some men have sailed the seas solo
> For other men space was their goal
> Some men have cameled 'cross deserts
> Some men have dived oceans deep
> Some men have plumbed noisome caverns
> And some through dense jungles did creep
> But despite their great feats of endurance
> Their stout hearts would quiver and quail
> At the thought (not too nice)
> Of the south polar ice
> Where a desperate man
> With a loo roll in hand
> Tries to squat in a ninety knot gale !

13   The Long-Drop

As I changed back into respectable tent wear I thought, that's one up on the usual "loo experience" stories that seemed mandatory at family gatherings back in England.   Then I remembered there was a better one.   The loo at Halley was something special and had enjoyed a notoriously special construction.

It was late January 1967 and six of Halley Bay's seven huts were erected. Fids due to leave Halley had already sailed and the second year fids plus we fidlets were now permanently ensconced, sleeping either at the old base or in the lofts of the new one pending the construction of bunk rooms. Sanitation inevitably became an issue so work on the seventh hut was postponed while a team of us tackled the problem of latrines. Flushing loos were clearly impracticable in the subzero temperatures, and a "long-drop" under a major hut would not only be impossible to excavate, it would also destabilise the hut. It was decided to construct a separate loo hut, that would be accessible from all the others via the main corrugated iron connecting tunnel.

The loo detail included John Gallsworthy, David Hill, Mike Skidmore, Big Al Smith and myself, though others too helped from time to time. Work commenced by digging an eight foot square hole but this quickly got too deep for us to throw out the shovels of snow so over the hole we erected a gantry that housed a pulley system. A rope was passed over the pulley and a topless forty five gallon drum attached; the other end was hooked to the tow hook of a Muskeg tractor. Pairs of us took it in turns to descend the deepening shaft in the oil drum, shovel ice into it and watch it being winched to the surface and emptied.

All went very well for forty two feet... then someone, with little understanding of physics, suggested we light a fire in a five gallon oil drum and it would melt its way down! I recall reminding folks that hot air rises, it does not sink, and as only the surface of the oil would burn, the bottom of the oil drum would remain pretty cold - "*ipso facto,* no hole," I summarised. Suffice it to say I was overruled but, understandably someone then said, "it's a big hole, why not use a big drum?".

Another forty five galloner was sought, stuffed about a third full with various waste combustibles and duly lowered into the pit.   A torch of oil soaked wood shavings and packaging was then ignited and ceremoniously dropped down the shaft.   I don't recall whether the first attempt was successful but the drum was soon burning nicely, sedately, a good brazier for a night watchman. At this point "Dad" Etchells got involved and kept feeding us with what he called "spent" oil. There was a lot of it and it didn't look very spent to me but I was determined to spend it again!

We started by pouring a pint or two at a time down the pit but the drop was so far, and the flames grown so big, that the stuff commenced igniting before reaching the bottom. We got more adventurous: half a gallon went down, then a gallon. It was all very exciting and great fun.

It was about then that Dad handed me a bucket with about five gallons and I trudged towards the pit intending to decant the stuff into smaller portions, but just as I neared the edge I tripped on the loose winch rope and the bucket and all five gallons went down below. I landed with head and shoulders overhanging the pit so had a good, if too close a view. Self preservation took over and having just registered the flaming depths like a scene worthy of Heronimous Bosch, I rolled aside as the first explosion occurred.

A flame hurtled up the shaft and licked around the gantry producing a vast cloud of black smoke and ensuring that we would need a new pulley attachment. Then it was as though the film went into reverse: there was the gasp of a giant drawing breath, and the flame and smoke disappeared back down the shaft. Almost at once there was a second explosion and the whole cycle was repeated, flame, smoke, then subglacial inhalation leaving the sky clear of smoke again. Wow, that was something, but it wasn't finished.

Five more times the fuel remnants exploded as they pistoned up and down the shaft and four more times smoke and flames were sucked back down into the abyss, each explosion and each cloud decreasing in size. The seventh and final blow allowed a small black cloud to drift quietly away over the base. At this point Ricky Chinn, our Base Commander, appeared. He was obviously spending far too long in the office as his face was very white! "I think we'd better leave it at that," he suggested with trembling voice. I concurred with an equal tremble.

Several hours later when the fuel drum had expired and everything had cooled we re-rigged the pulley and descended with a tape measure. From 42 feet we had indeed deepened the pit to 43 feet 6 inches! But from eight feet square it was now an impressive thirteen feet diameter in the lower half.

The story, the one-upmanship on loos does not end there. I recall the shocked report of an elderly aunt who encountered a French "squatter" for the first time, and the equally shocked account from an uncle who had had to use an Italian urinal in view of ladies who were entering their toilets. Loos at Halley were also basic and functional.

Across the top of the newly dug long-drop long joists were laid on which was constructed the loo hut. This was subdivided into three compartments, two were made into cubicles, each occupying a quarter of the area and fitted with "sit downers". These were simply five gallon oil drums that had been topped and tailed and fastened over appropriately sized holes cut in the floor. We did have the luxury of wooden seats crafted by the chippies (carpenters), though it was strange that amongst the generous supply of sinks, washbasins, showers and chairs of all types send from England, no one had thought to include a single loo seat! The remaining area of the loo hut had two more holes in the floor, one of these had two five galloners, one on top of the other, as a urinal, the other hole was topped by a forty five gallon drum down which the kitchen "gash" was dumped - general slops and food scrapings, though there was never much of the latter.

Although the cubicles had doors, speed not privacy was the rule. In fact it was wise to try to time one's sit to a quiet period when others might not need the urinals or no gash was due. The problem was that all holes opened to the one great drop and one could be sitting comfortably when a colleague might enter the outer area. His opening and closing the door (or worse dumping gash down the chute), pumped air down the nearest holes... and back up the cubicle loos... air that had been supercooling below for some time! It was no place to sit and contemplate the meaning of life as one was in danger of losing one's fundamental principles.

Eventually, after a year or more, there developed, or rather grew, an unwelcome intrusion into our loos. Things were coming to a head (or more exactly to a bottom - indeed all bottoms) as rather unpleasant brown stalagmites were growing alarmingly from the depths. This generated serious discussion one smoko but first on the agenda there had to be an agreement on terminology. A rhyming two syllable word combining old English and the latter half of "stalagmite" was suggested. Considering its geological correctness and the poetic aspect it was perhaps the best term, but it was also felt to be a little too, shall we say, "direct"; something marginally more genteel or subtle was sought. "Turdicle" was felt to reflect the ambience, even though it was upstanding and not pedunculate.

When our base commander eventually directed us to action not philosophy, it was suggested that we should shoot the offending columns with the base rifle. At this point Murray Roberts, our doc, said the blast in a confined space could damage the ear drums. A quieter method was therefore sought and a felling axe suggested, but this necessitated someone descending to undertake the fell deed - but who?

All eyes turned on me as not only the General Assistant, but also the guy with climbing experience, and the guy who had earned his glowing nickname installing the lights in the loo (a triple whammy).

Accepting my true station in life I declined the axe and armed myself with a lump hammer instead. I screwed a strong hook into a roof timber over the gash drum and suspended a climbing rope. Then after rigging myself with harness and prussiks (rope climbing clamps) - and putting a "do not use" notice on the door - I descended the abyss. Half way down, I accidentally spun on the rope and knocked lightly against one turdicle, whereupon it totally collapsed, so I swung gently and kicked the other causing it to collapse also. Hence, job done without resorting to demolition tools, and feeling quite smug, I resurfaced and we all looked forward to a couple of years of comfortable contemplations.

My second descent was a little more traumatic and had nothing to do with turdicles; indeed the fact that turdicles were not involved should have been a warning. It was January '69 and the Perla Dan relief ship had docked on the sea ice. I was due to embark but wanted a few more photographs before doing so. On one tractor trip to the ship, I bought half a dozen films but lacked a bag to put them in, so carried them back to my bunk room in the crook of my arm.

En route I passed the loo and, being desperate, called in, only to watch one of my films fall down the pee hole. Undaunted, and now a self professed expert on loo descents, I re-rigged the tackle (and the notice) and descended once more. There was the film at the bottom, plain to see; I just needed one step across to pick it up. Fortunately a recollection of the previous occasion at last flashed in mind and I glanced around nostalgically before stepping out of the prussik. But where were the turdicles? Surely they would be starting to grow again, or even just the remnants of my earlier exploit should be scattered like Greek ruins.

Nothing… and then I realised my film was not "lying" at the bottom, it was "floating". One might say that was the nearest I ever came to being "in turd" before my time! Interesting scientific note that the "long-drop" contents melted in summer despite being inside a deep freeze.

•   •   •

Out on the plateau things were getting tough too. The temperature was down to thirty below freezing and there was an unusual damp feeling in the air that gave that raw English winter feel, but much colder. The accompanying wind was, as my old granny used to say, a "lazy wind": doesn't bother going round but goes straight through you. The snow surface also deteriorated and the dogs found the going difficult causing our daily mileage to deteriorate too. And then we received a radioed answer to our proposal about the direct route to the Shacks.

"Sorry lads, but London says no. They don't want us to waste another season."

The timing and the wording could have been better chosen. After the initial anger, pen went straight to paper:

There are eighteen crates of field gear
        at a depot near the Shacks,
There's another dump of goodies on the way;
To north and south of both of these,
        two fifty miles of tracks,
That were reccied by some lads from Halley Bay;
There's cairns and drums and flags and things
        arranged in careful lines,
To facilitate the finding of each spot,
But two years snow obliterates
        most prominent of signs,
And so, you see, we'll lose the bloody lot!

The Eliason or "Elsan" motor toboggan
(a rough idea and apologies to experts!)

14   Fids in Wonderland

"It's most odd," I commented to Mike as we traversed the high plateau between the Therons and the Brunt Ice Shelf, "most odd."

Mike was quizzical.

"Well, I keep thinking we'll get a better view when we get over that next rise but we've been travelling all morning and that next rise is just as far away; despite the fact that every next flag seems to be near the top!" I then looked astern and on both sides: "In fact, there are rises in every direction. It's as though we're sledging in a basin.   And what's more we're permanently in the bottom!"

It was true.   The day was beautiful, the sky clear except for the fine ice crystals that reflected the sunlight, forming a fine sun pillar.   The snow was excellent: crisp, hard and clear of awkward sastrugi.   Plate crystals winked and flashed as we drove past.

The dogs were running well too.   I knew Whisky, my lead dog was due to retire on arrival at Halley, so I was trying other possibilities.   Chalky was still too flighty and distracted by the eight males behind her, though she did run well alongside Whisky in the first days of her leader training.   Shem had been tried and although there was a degree of promise, he seemed too immature... perhaps next year.

It was wonderful years later to read in a 1973 report that "Shem, the old bugger, has been transferred to Stonington." Shem had always been a favourite and I still have his portrait, painted by Mike, but I could never think of him as old.

Changi and Luqa were similarly too young and still needed leading though Changi was showing signs of responding to commands and not just following. Stroma and Skye, the old boys were my low gear and often ran with slack traces on fast surfaces and today boasted one such surface. Like Whisky, the old lads would be retired soon.

That left only Wensen and Esk and of the two Esk seemed the dominant, though the most awkward and bad tempered. Nevertheless, since re-spanning, his attitude had improved considerably and we now gave him a try up front. I think both Mike and I were quite surprised at the success, though like anyone given new responsibility, whether dog or human, there is always some anxiety and a looking back for reassurance.

But here, in the middle of that amazing polar basin, Esk was doing fine.

I considered the basin effect again.

While commuting between the old base and the Village I had often been surprised to see several icebergs way out to sea. Once, as Colin Wornham and I stood on the steel track guards of our Muskeg transport, I had remarked not only on our ability to see the icebergs long before we got near a cliff top but also on their apparent height. "They look to be much taller than the local cliffs," I observed, "and I feel to be looking up at them." In fact I had the distinct feeling I was looking up at the sea itself. We must be going downhill, I mused, and we can see beyond the cliff line; but I knew the shelf ice on which we were travelling was flat... we should not be able to see the sea or anything on it.

"Mirage," said Colin succinctly, the engine noise discouraging further conversation. I wasn't certain whether he was giving a scientific explanation or commenting on my imagination so I thought it over.

Most people are familiar with mirages, not the giant

standpipe in the middle of the Sahara tempting thirst crazed travellers with a constant drip, but the common summer mirages seen on many a hot beach or open road. The appearance is of a pool of water just below the horizon and we *know* it's water because any car in the vicinity is reflected on the surface!

At the other end of the temperature scale over the polar ice, mirages can also be seen. These polar mirages are technically known as "superior mirages", as opposed to the "inferior mirages" that form over hot surfaces. I needed a little mild physics to help the digestion though perhaps my old physics teacher would have criticised the detail.

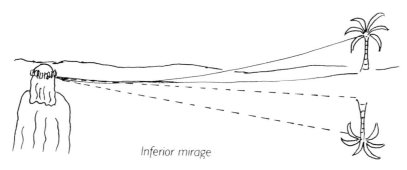

Inferior mirage

When light passes from warm air to cold air at a shallow angle (or from cold to warm) it bends noticeably away from the "hotter" layers. (The terms "hot", "warm" & "cold" are purely relative to each other.) This means that light rays, say from the top of a palm tree, that start their journey obliquely towards the hot desert sand some distance away will enter the hotter air near the ground and be bent back up. Rays from the bottom of the tree starting out parallel to the ground are already in the hottest air so do not bend as much. Of course our brains cannot detect the bends so we see the top of the tree below the ground level, and because of its lesser bending ray the tree bottom looks to be above its top… upside down. We also see the direct rays (not shown in the diagram) so there are two trees, one the right way up, the other upside down. Finally we see the sky behind the miraged tree so the whole thing looks like the reflection of a tree in what our brain assumes to be water. I mean, it can't be sky below ground can it? Its obviously a reflection in a lake!

Conversely light from the top of an iceberg that starts heading slightly upwards is bent back towards the colder air at the surface. The result of this being that the iceberg looks to be not only up in the sky but much taller than it really is.

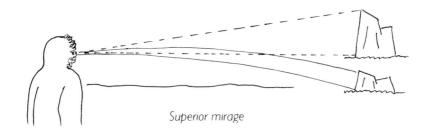

Superior mirage

Here was my answer to the Halley Bay iceberg puzzle. Colin had said "mirage" and mirage it was. Light from the icebergs, in fact from the whole seascape, was bending over the cold shelf ice allowing us to see not just the entire 'berg but a much taller version. Colin and I hadn't been commuting down a slope, the icebergs had taken to the skies! Another amazing aspect of this "superior mirage" is that one can often see distant objects above an intervening one that would normally hide it from view.

Here also was the answer to another phenomenon, our seeing the Shackleton Range from the Slessor Glacier at a distance of sixty to seventy miles, even though the mountains were only a few hundred metres higher than the plateau on which we travelled. Miraging was also the answer to sledging in a basin. The horizon in every direction was a superior mirage of itself making it look considerably higher.

• • •

Relieved that there was no serious slope to climb we sledged on, enjoying the beautiful day and trying out a newly composed sledging song based on an old Gracie Fields melancholy number. It seemed appropriate in view of the earlier radio message but the beauty of the day transferred any potential melancholy into humour (just like Gracie).

> We've wasted our time all this summer
> So next year just where will we go?
> The answer is plain so just sing this refrain
> Out in the cold, cold snow.

There were plenty more verses where that came from!

Atmospheric conditions often caused me to genuinely rejoice in pleasure or wonder or both. As I sit typing in my very English cottage, I can see a couple of dogs in the distance, not huskies nor any canine breed, these dogs lack teeth, tails and even legs but they are brightly coloured; they are "sun dogs" or in scientific parlance "parhelia". Often thought to be reserved for polar climes, they are very common in temperate latitudes and I frequently see them in English skies.

Sun dogs are bright rainbow coloured patches that form in the sky 22° either side of the sun if there is a suitable thin layer of high cloud composed of ice crystals. Those crystals refract the sun's rays, and just as sun on rain produces rainbows, so also sun on ice crystals produces the same rainbow colours. They are easily missed simply because you have to look quite close to a bright sun but once you have seen a good one, they are not forgotten. Sun dogs, sun halos and sun pillars (a column of brightly lit ice crystals ascending through the sun) were all very common phenomena at Halley but I never failed to delight in them.

There, because of the super clean air, ice crystals often floated independently not forming visible clouds, which made their effect on the sun's rays more apparent and more pure. It was on the high plateau during a tractor expedition that my enthusiasm for parhelic displays was rewarded.

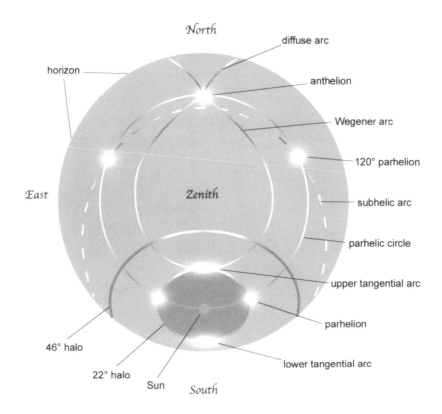

Parhelic display seen on the high plateau

NB the positions of East and West are not wrong, remember you are looking up!
Try holding the diagram overhead and aligning the page with true north.

The sky was totally clear of visible cloud and consequently a luxurious deep blue. Strangely, the sky inside a sun halo is, or seems to be, darker than that outside and it was perhaps this effect that first caught my attention as I drove the big International tractor directly towards the sun. Should be good sun dogs I thought, and there were, but there was more, far more. I shouted to the others and we all gazed aloft, some in awe, some bemused, some incredibly with little interest. The display filled the sky and I had to lay on my back in the snow to see how it all fitted together. It was the only time I regretted not having bought that expensive "fisheye" lens in Port Stanley!

To the south, the sun is housed inside a large full halo at 22° from the sun with another even bigger halo at 46°. This outer halo fills a quarter of our total horizon and a third of the dome overhead. Running horizontally through the sun, a bright line continues right round the horizon, a complete encircling band of light called a "parhelic circle". To either side of the sun where the inner halo and parhelic circle meet, two dazzlingly bright full colour sun dogs. At the bottom of the same halo, a very bright line suggesting the start of downward tangential arc. At the top of the 22° halo a similar bright line but this then dims and continues in an upward arc that swings its two arms high over head and then both descend to meet the parhelic circle exactly opposite the sun and produce a slight brightening of the circle at that point - the "anthelion". Finally just to ensure east and west are not deprived, a "subhelic circle" (which we can't actually see today) crosses the parhelic circle 120° from the sun, on each side, to create two more sun dogs (which we can see) as bright splashes of colour.

Strangely, though Halley is renowned for the quality and frequency of Auroral displays, and though I regularly had to go outside the base in the winter months, I never, in the whole two years, saw a good Aurora Australis! Nevertheless, the summer parhelic displays more than compensated and on that high plateau they put a song in my heart: it was time to write another, but as I write, it is a different rhyme that comes to mind, a poem triggered by another aerial memory.

One bright clear day as we snow bound ants had been crawling past the Theron Mountains, a speedier form of transport was seen high in the sky. It was a straight winged, four engined aircraft of distinctive shape: a Lockheed C130 transport plane. A plane was the last thing we expected to see over the Antarctic ice cap but we assumed it was heading for the one of the American bases at either the South Pole or McMurdo on the other side of the continent. It was, but at the time we did not know that both it, and an unnoticed companion C130, were flying from Halley Bay! And nor did we know they were a rescue mission taking a seriously injured man to hospital.

Mobster Creek and the penguin rookery were earning a bad reputation for dangerous happenings and one day in early 1968, Doc John Brotherhood, he of the three hour tooth extraction, with Jim Shirtcliffe, builder and carpenter of several years Antarctic experience, were out manhauling their loaded sledge en route for the penguin rookery. The weather worsened... but I'll let the poem tell the tale. And lest anyone feel that a serious accident should not be recorded so flippantly, Doc John was pleased and amused by my rendition. Lewis Carol fans will immediately recognise the style and meter which seemed perfect for this tale, especially when considering the cast: the doctor and the carpenter.

Liberal but gentle poetic licence is exercised and no criticism implied of any of the people involved who handled the whole affair with total competence. Doc John was skilfully tended and sheltered by his injured colleague. Base Commander Ricky Chin gets a little ribbing not because of any failing but because this was the year that Base Leaders were restyled "Commanders" and we all saluted and teased the poor guy. The "we" references are also poetic license as, being beside the Slessor Glacier at the time, I was obviously not on base to take part in the events. Nevertheless how do you evacuate a seriously injured casualty? - or more to the point, how does an inexperienced ground crew make a runway for a four engined C130 transport plane?

The sun was shining on the ice,
    shining with all his might
Which may seem odd because it was
    the middle of the night
But midnight suns in polar lands
    are really quite all right.

The sky was blue, as blue could be,
    the snow was white and clean
And every little crystal glinted
    pink and gold and green
And no crevasses marred the track,
    at least none to be seen.

A mile or two from Halley Bay,
    where sea and shelf ice meet,
There was a wall of gleaming cliffs,
    in height a hundred feet,
And on a wondrous day as this,
    the scene was quite a treat.

The doctor and the carpenter
    were walking close at hand
To see those cliffs, they both agreed,
    indeed it would be grand
Right manfully they hauled their sledge
    towards the frozen strand.

"The day is fine," the doctor said,
    "Indeed it is quite warm."
They did not notice to the east,
    great cloud banks start to form
And all too soon they were engulfed
    within a polar storm.

Too late they headed back to base,
    but quite soon lost the track
They veered too far, stepped off the cliff
    (a compass they did lack)
The carpenter was quite cut up,
    the doctor broke his back.

The sledge with their survival kit
    had landed close beside,
So painfully, the carpenter,
    this crucial load untied,
Then bravely pitched the polar tent
    and dragged the doc inside.

On base the lads were panicking:
    the loo door was badly bent,
The carpenter was needed,
    so a rescue team was sent,
Eventually the two were found,
    both "loitering within tent".

"Ironic this," the doctor said,
    "In fact it is quite thick,
"Cos, I'm the one who should stay well,
    "To tend the lame and sick."
The carpenter said nothing but
    "It was stupid trick!"

The two were carried back with care,
    (a tricky enterprise)
The carpenter was patched up,
    and bed rest then advised,
The doctor needed X-rays which we took…
    he supervised.

The base commander then took charge, and said
    "I'll send you home".
'Til someone gently said to him
    that all the ships had gone.
"Let's send an SOS," he said,
    "You know it could be fun."

Then two days on a drone was heard,
    from way up in the sky,
The lads dashed out and looked about:
    two planes approached on high,
Across the Polar continent,
    the Yanks had dared to fly.

Just then one pilot phoned the base:
    "Is anyone to hand?
"I must admit, from where I sit,
    your place looks really grand,
"Oh by the way, could you mark out,
    a place for me to land?"

The base commander scratched his head
    and said, "We're in a stew"
The base commander scratched his head
    and said, "What can we do?"
As though to say to all who heard,
    he hadn't got a clue.

With cunning look, in came the cook,
    and whispered in his ear
Reminding him of surplus stores,
    that got shipped down each year
They'd half a ton of cocoa left,
    'cos all they drank was beer.

"The very thing," the leader said,
    "Now we can get a grip,
"And there's a silver lining
    to our doctors sorry slip,
"We'll rid ourselves of cocoa
    as we mark a landing strip."

With happy shout, the lads dashed out,
    and really went to town,
And made a brand new runway,
    outlined in chocolate brown,
And then we stood and waited as
    one rescue plane touched down.

The second plane, the escort flight,
    had nothing much to do,
For safety's sake, their orders were
    to circle in the blue
But after such a lengthy flight…
    did no one need the loo?

The aircrew were made welcome,
    by our many chocolate grins,
We gave them hospitality,
    of coffee, tea and gins,
We could not offer cocoa
    'cos we'd emptied all the tins.

The pilot said the landing strip
     was quite the best one going,
But smiled and then apologised,
     for he'd assumed our knowing
"A simple fire," he said, "would show,
     which way the wind was blowing".

With jet assisted take off,
     the plane gave lots of power,
Which blew the cocoa all about,
     and made the lads quite sour,
So everyone then trooped inside
     and lined up for the shower.

The doctor made the long flight home,
     his full recovery sure,
The carpenter, he stayed on base,
     to mend that broken door,
You may think that's the end on that...
     but there was one thing more.

A fortnight on, a keen young lad,
     with hearing quite acute,
Said, "There's a plane," and dashed outside,
     we followed, hot pursuit
Large boxes were descending,
     beneath a parachute.

Anticipation mounted
     for the contents of those freights
Presents from our loved ones?
     letters from our mates?
But all we got was cocoa,
     about a dozen crates!

The last line is most unfair, we did get presents and letters from home as well as a new supply of magazines and other goodies from the Americans at McMurdo Base. In fact much of the poem is unfair on the characters: the carpenter pitched the tent over the doctor so as not to cause further injury by moving him and the rescue was mounted for genuinely humane reasons, the loo door was perfectly ok!

My Sledge Bag
with team name "Hairy Breeks"
my call sign "AKE"
and the Yorkshire Rose

15   Frozen Assets

"Bugger me! Look at me beer!" That must have been the exclamation (or something similar) when the unnamed fid at the old base prized off the bottle cap and attempted to poor a glass of best bitter...

The strange thing about living in a freezer - for our average outdoor temperature was several degrees lower than that of a domestic deep freeze - was that normal concepts about food storage had to be reversed. A sledge load of meat or eggs or anything else that "goes off" in plus temperatures could be left unloaded for weeks: all year if need be. True the resultant fried egg did look rather odd, rather like a small yellow snooker ball on a thin white sheet of plastic, but while they lasted they tasted good. Unfortunately eggs didn't last very long, nothing delectable would have done if the cooks had not kept a tight reign on supplies. Though we all appreciated their prudence on the special occasions when wonderful meals with puddings and amazing cakes were served, there were times when a genuine scrambled or fried egg would have gone down extremely well.

Actually, egg we did have in quite plentiful supply: the dried powder variety, probably ex-War Department left over from 1945, but it didn't look appetising on toast or with a slice of bacon. The result of the fresh egg shortage was evident when, after our two years of near deprivation we embarked on the Perla Dan. The ship's cook enquired solicitously for our choice of first meal: "Eggs," was the unanimous reply... an answer I suspect he anticipated. I managed twelve without much effort, John Gallsworthy devoured eighteen!

One good aspect of the outdoor freezer was that on tractor expeditions we could take boxes of bread rolls, freshly baked on base, and simply thaw them out in the heated tractor cab when needed. Meat and fish were also a welcome addition to a monotonous field menu.

At the opposite end of the polar perishable food spectrum were canned foods and anything containing liquids that would freeze. Tinned beans and greens were hurriedly stored in the capacious loft above the kitchen and dining room, the limited beer ration (two cans on a Saturday night) was secreted above the bar, which was also adjacent to the base commanders office!

This dismal supply was often supplemented by private orders, made by radio, to our office at Port Stanley in the Falkland Islands. Crates would then be sent with the next relief ship from one of the two pubs: the "Globe" or the "Ship", whichever had been preferred during our brief sojourn on the voyage south. Several of we fids were quite astounded at the significant "cairn" of crates that attended the order of our diesel mechanic, John "JC" Carter. It seemed like the supply of an obviously serious drinker, either that or he was about to throw several generous parties. A quick calculation however demonstrated that his mountain of booze, that had to last a full year, permitted JC less than one bottle per day, somewhat less than his UK intake. He guarded that supply keenly and jealously, and rare and lucky the man to be offered a glass.

Beer should have become a valuable trading item but because the ration was so minimal and everyone partook, and also because all personal supplies were so precious, it did not enter the stock market. The main currency that fluctuated dramatically was "nutty" - chocolate to non-fids. We were allocated individual bimonthly rations of four boxes: Dairy Milk, Bournville, Whole Nut and Caramello, each box containing a dozen bars. In reality this was over generous and rarely consumed in total by people on base, though one of our team was heard to exclaim on receiving his four box ration:

"Ooh goody, two more days of bliss!". Field men were also keen to receive their ration but much was carefully stored to supplement the meagre sledging supplies.

As the sledging season approached, these field men could be seen in surreptitious negotiations with meteorologists, ionosphericists, cooks and others due to stay on base. There would be the transfer of socks, chamois or silk gloves, a sweater perhaps, and said field man would scurry away with another box or two and a satisfied grin. Inevitably, the perceived need was disproportionate to the actual consumption which led to an attempt at resale towards the end of the field season. By this time of course the bottom had dropped out of the market and it was not unknown for surplus chocolate to be left at field depots for future parties.

There were two other items of valued currency which though traded rarely, retained their commercial value: sledging anoraks and sweaters. The long, double thickness ventile anoraks came in grey, orange or green and sported the luxurious wolverine fur round the hood. They were obviously far too good to be wasted in use at Halley for they would single a young man out on the streets of London or Manchester: "Look, there's a real explorer!" would be the hoped for exclamation of some young maiden, or several, let's not be pessimistic.

A second design of anorak was also issued, the "base anorak". This was single thickness, shorter and had no wolverine fur. It was in reality a very useful garment for most outdoor jobs as the longer sledging anoraks would often hamper one's work, and incredibly, the fur was uncomfortable round the neck when the hood was not required. I used my base anorak for significant periods even while sledging as I found the latter variety too warm and cumbersome.

Yes, sledging anoraks were ideally destined for the UK "goodies box". Nevertheless, there were annual complaints about the base anorak! In my "clothing report" to London HQ after I had been put in charge of field equipment and clothing, I observed:

> "A mild bone of contention regarding base anoraks. In all seriousness I have come to believe that most people want a base anorak to be as warm and long as a sledging anorak for one reason only: they want to leave the sledging anorak untouched in the goodies box!"

As regards the sweaters, these were similarly preserved. Fids would again complain loud and long that their issue of three rather attractive woollen sweaters for two years was inadequate. After eighteen months or so I would be shown a tatty garment with frayed cuffs and holes in the elbows: "See they're no good!" would be the exclamation. As the complainants only ever wore their one disintegrating sweater one presumed that a couple of pristine woollies lined their goodies box!

There were other complaints against the BAS clothing, mostly trivial and expressing preferences rather than need, but as the formal kit issue to fids was undertaken in Port Stanley there was little chance to adjust or add. Big Al was justly named and at over twenty one stones (135 kg) he was worried that the standard issue would not fit. He had expressed his concern before leaving England only to be met with the a rather supercilious response: "We've fitted bigger men than you!"... They hadn't. Fortunately Al's wife had kitted him out herself with the result that he had the best shirts and least scratchy trousers on base.

As a GA I knew I would be dealing with the dogs which included their feeding. Talk in Port Stanley had been of seal gutting and the need for a good seal knife. This was in the days when it was considered not just acceptable but essential to feed dogs on seal meat; in the days when dogs themselves were considered acceptable in the Antarctic!

"You'll need a *good* knife," said one old fid as I carried my brand new kit back to the ship. He stressed the word "good" as he cynically glanced at my BAS issue sealing knife complete with sharpening steel. I queried its inadequacies.

"No shape to the handle; too easy for your hand to slide onto the blade and slice yourself; end up with 'seal finger' ", he didn't explain the term but it sounded unpleasant. "Blade's too short and it won't take a good edge..." It appeared I had a totally useless piece of equipment so promptly sought a good hardware shop in town. If I had been better advised I need not have bothered for the purchased knife's first real airing was some years later, slicing bread on a family camping holiday in the Lake District!

What I should have been told was that we would not be shooting, gutting and cutting seal meat as needed, we would be taking on a year's supply of carcasses at South Georgia to be cut up on base. The consequence of this was, like all other meat, by the time we needed them the seals were frozen solid. A five inch sheath knife to a frozen elephant seal is as a plastic pick to granite quarry. The only way to get through that meat was by saw, a petrol driven power saw. Even the electric saw was inadequate. It was like cutting wet oak. Seal knife! I suspect that old fid had lived exclusively on the Grahamland bases where fresh seal was readily available. He didn't know the meaning of "cold" I later mused smugly.

"Just look at me beer!" exclaimed that perhaps apocryphal fid a second time to encourage the requisite crowd.

Carrying a few precious bottles, he had just climbed the frost encrusted ladder from the fifteen metre depths of the IGY hut. The IGY hut had virtually been abandoned for there was no heating down there though it still contained some stores. No heat in a hut fifteen metres deep in Antarctic ice means cold, very cold... A bottle opener had been applied and the onlookers were now gathered round, amazed and amused: There, twixt bottle and glass, and captured like a photographic study of still life, was a frozen cataract of amber nectar.

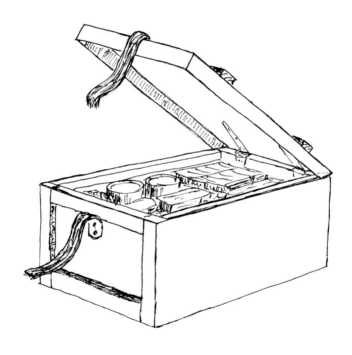

Sledge Box

*Containing expedition food
for two men for ten days*

16   Bob Pi

In November 1961, Denis Ardus and Colin Johnson set the example for exploratory travel at Halley, and kindled the dreams of many a doggyman by forging the first crossing of the deadly hinge zone between the floating shelf ice to the inland ice cap of Coats Land.   Not satisfied with that signal achievement they headed for some mountains that were now visible on the eastern horizon. In one journey they pioneered a complete dog route from Halley to the Tottanfjella, an unexplored mountain range. Although a food and fuel depot was established for them on the ice shelf just short of the hinge zone, their run of over 700 miles return with one dog team, remains the longest unaccompanied expedition of any kind ever run from Halley.

The problem and danger of the hinge zone that they had negotiated which such skill and aplomb, was the result of three natural occurrences: in addition to the Brunt Ice Shelf rotating about the south west corner and producing those very convenient creeks at the coast, ice floats, and there are tides in the Antarctic Ocean. The consequence of these factors being that the Brunt Shelf rises and falls with the tide. Where the non-tidal inland ice becomes the floating shelf there is a hinge, an enormous hinge around two hundred metres deep and ten to fifteen miles wide, wider the further one travels into the faster moving ice to the east. Such a hinge in ice does not articulate smoothly like a door hinge but produces a series of great cracks or crevasses. Ardus and Johnson forced a route through this hinge but it was not suitable for heavier vehicles and a new crossing was required.

The challenge was answered in part, in January 1962 when Alan Precious in company with David Easty, Eric Jones and John Skilling found another potentially safer route further west. This route, which perhaps should have born the title of the "Precious Crossing" (and it was an extremely precious find) earned a different name…

One Sunday two months later Bob Lee and Mike "Pi" Jarman (the nickname rather depended on being spelled Py but he was a mathematician and preferred Pi) set out for a drive in a Muskeg. They approximately followed the Alan Precious route and found themselves at the top of the ice slope at the far side of the hinge zone. One account suggests they left a small depot and the route was initially referred to as the crossing to Bob and Pi's depot, but others suggest that the lads had no supplies to make a depot… they were on a Sunday jolly. All agree however that it was a scandalously hazardous trip and they were lucky to return without incident. Perhaps it was their sheer audacity that ensured their names be remembered, for the "Bob Pi Crossing" it became and was so known and used for the next dozen years or so.

The "Bob Pi" was, during the 60s, suitable for tractors… with care… with great care. The line through the crevasses was flagged at every twist and turn, and accurate navigation notes taken for use by subsequent travellers; it was also soon extended to the top of the exit slope that climbed to the ice cap. Nevertheless, the whole region was constantly on the move with new crevasses opening, old ones widening or occasionally disappearing, all of which required regular checking and adjusting before every major expedition.

Flag 36, in the early '60s terminology, was at the top of the final slope. Originally it had been the thirty sixth and last flag of the Bob Pi route but later re-routings gave the place other numbers. This led to minor confusion, so, as the depot that was established there was en-route to several destinations, we renamed it Crossroads: Turn left for the Tottanfjella and the Heimfrontfjella, turn right for the Dawson Lambton Ice Stream a strange tongue of ice projecting into the Weddell Sea, straight on for the Therons and Shackletons.

· · ·

Our arrival at Crossroads Depot on the return from the Shackleton recce denoted the end of the plateau, the end of the inland ice. Halley Bay was still some fifty miles away and we could see the huts through binoculars. Short though the distance was in comparison to that covered to date, the most dangerous section lay ahead. The route dipped noticeably down the three three mile slope towards the Bob Pi Crossing. I felt I knew the crossing for I had already traversed it twice with dogs and three times with tractors but it was a place where familiarity bred caution not contempt. Discovering a crevasse the careless way can be sudden, dramatic, painful and final. Generally the crevasses run parallel to the subglacial coast but not always. ie. the bottom of the exit slope, but perhaps the rotation of the ice shelf, or maybe simply the complex tensions within a ten mile wide hinge, cause other crevasses to open at almost any angle to the general line. And crevasses, whatever their direction, can be big... very big. Some we estimated at fifteen metres wide but these tended to have almost refilled with snow making them more like ice valleys with a perimeter of cliffs. Except in whiteout, these were easily seen and easily avoided. Some small cracks at several centimetres were relatively innocuous and did not concern us. Others, too wide to cross and unfathomably deep were also clearly visible and relatively easy to accommodate in route finding. The dangerous ones were wide enough to swallow a man, a sledge or even a whole tractor and were quite invisible.

On high mountain ridges, drifting snow swirls in vertical eddies forming large overhanging cornices. The same occurs along the side of a crevasse until the cornice reaches the far rim, or alternate winds generate cornices from both sides and they meet in the middle, hiding the bottomless void... a veritable mantrap.

After a period without snow accumulation, these coverings or "bridges" would settle a little and we could often discern the faint parallel shadows that marked the edge of a shallow sided depression. A depression that said beware, crevasse beneath.

Dropping the bridge of a crevasse with glaciologist Paul Coslett had been a sobering experience. Working in a contorted area of shelf east of Halley, we had probed for and perforated the edge of a depression with our long ice chisels. Nothing seemed to happen and I began to think that the bridge was too solid and thick to move, when suddenly a section ten to twenty metres long dropped out of view. Noiselessly at first then with a "whoomf" as the bridge either disintegrated or hit the bottom or... we never found out for all we could see was a blue black bottomless hole, wide enough and long enough to swallow us both, complete with dogs and sledge, without touching the sides. Colin Wornham with radar technician Brian Swift had had a fright in the same region the previous year when doggying out to set up a glaciological beacon. He writes:

"When almost there, the hills and valleys became more pronounced and whilst running down one descent, saw at the last minute a snow bridge over a big hole. Too late to stop or avoid it, the dogs raced over, we pulled hard on the skijoring lines in order to accelerate our own passage, but the back of the loaded sledge crashed through the bridge and the front reared up. With our frantic shouts of "vheet-

vheet-vheet" there was just sufficient power and momentum to prevent the sledge from dragging us and dogs down into the hole - certainly never to be seen again. It was a crevasse about six feet wide and bottomless. We rated it a 'near miss'! We took a rather different route and considerably more care on our return trip."

Often, such crevasse-indicating depressions were not apparent, either because there had been little subsidence or the sunlight was too diffuse to produce shadows. For this reason, travel through the hinge zone of the Bob Pi was an extremely dangerous undertaking in whiteout or after new snow. It was dangerous enough in good visibility on a well settled surface for it required a twenty mile twisting route through the crevassing to traverse the ten mile wide hinge. In reality it was a rather large deeply exaggerated "S" bend that steered between two enormous overlapping chasms but the route was crossed in several places by other smaller chasms and crevasses: not a totally comfortable place to be.

> The tell tale crystal byway,
> Smooth and straight the track,
> Laid by no man, trod by no foot,
> Deep wintered between white verges,
> Road to adventure?
> Road to oblivion.
> A tap, a probe with the long ice chisel…
> An indigo eye blinks open
> And from dark unfathomable void
> Gazes softly up at me,
> Taunting me, tempting me.
> "Come closer! come and follow!"
> Thus speaks the silent seduction.

But what am I you one-eyed hag?
A fool?
Your enchantment is that of a sorceress
Luring me to your embrace
To chance delight against disaster
To dice with abyssal death;
For of old do I know you:
Silent siren of the snow!
Veiled, your gaping maw,
Cloaked, your cavernous belly,
Masked, your teeth of shining crystal,
Sharp and hungry for innocent traveller.
And yet…

Within that innocent, murderous stare,
A glimpse, a hint of beauty.
I will slice away your face of falsehood,
Strike off your mantle of deceit,
I will lay you naked to the sky.
And pluck the icy treasures from your deeps
Let the sun play his iridescent rays
Upon your fine cut glass
Your chiming chandeliers,
Your diadems
That no Dutch diamond cutter could equal.

How can such joy, such wonder
Be entombed in such a place of dread
You blue black pit,
You mantrap,
You crevasse.

As we sped down the Bop Pi slope to the crossing below I tried to see the route ahead but we were still two or three miles from the hinge itself and the route flags were very small. The slope was almost a broad valley for on either side were prominent bluffs, protruding towards the shelf below. Both bluffs were riddled with enormous crevasses; ours was the only way down.

Stroma, long recovered from his chaffing and sore toes was enjoying the run. Thinking him to be the slowest member of the team and not needing full strength downhill, and perhaps more importantly, not wanting the sledge to run him down, we cast him adrift as we commenced the descent. Bless the old fellow; he didn't want to feel unwanted and soon rejoined the team, trotting along in his rightful place next to his brother Skye. At the bottom I re-harnessed him as I didn't want him to suffer the same fate as poor Medina on last years Therons reconnaissance when she went AWOL from one of the teams. Perhaps the cause was her being "on heat", whatever, Medina had slipped her harness and created chaos amongst the male dogs but she could not be caught nor cajoled back with dog food. After three days of no Nutrican she did manage to catch and eat a lone, unusual, unwary and very unlucky bird, a Snowy Petrel. After another day she decided to go home and was last seen heading back along the sledge tracks towards Halley Bay. Unfortunately the route lay through the Bob Pi crevasses. The tractor party that followed the dog teams some days later reported seeing a lone animal's tracks in the crevasse field. Tracks that ended at the edge of a very large hole. There were no paw prints at the other side and none turning back... I could imagine that poor beast, for annoying though she must have been, I hated to contemplate her fate. She must have been pretty miserable, certainly very hungry, and head down, just keeping going when suddenly there was nothing in front of her, just oblivion below.

A lone dog is vulnerable, just as is a lone man, but a team of dogs with a driver was considered the safest way to negotiate crevassed terrain. Enter a crevassed zone with a Skidoo or tractor and the first thing to find a hole is the machine itself, complete with the driver. With dogs and careful driving, one can stop even if a dog falls through a bridge, and provided he is still in his harness one can pull him out, usually unhurt. This was the view I held for many years until learning of a later accident, but whatever the transport, it was always prudent to probe ahead for crevasses.

On one recce of the Bob Pi this probing ahead produced an amusing or scary incident, depending on one's point of view. I had spotted a suspicious groove some thirty centimetres wide. It lay across the bottom of a slight depression. I grasped the crevasse probe, left my colleague with the team and slowly skied ahead, probing as I went. Sure enough, the first probe at the edge of the groove went straight through and a deep blue eye gazed up at me. I leaned forward and probed the middle and the far side. Yes, all hollow so to make sure of its limit I cleared both sides back to the edges and was relieved to find it was no wider underneath than the groove on top. I then backed off and called over my shoulder, "deep but easily crossable," and then... "bugger me!"

We had all grown accustomed to the old wooden skis that were perfect for crevasse work. They spread one's load as a ski should, they slid when required as a ski should, but they also had a certain inertia due to the rarely waxed wooden sole which meant one could "stick" on moderate slopes. The mid 1960's saw the introduction of plastic composite skis and we were now using them for the first time. As I backed away from the crevasse up the slight incline, my backward glance must have unweighted the skis for I found myself sliding gracefully, slowly downhill, to stop perfectly bridged across the hole. Space beneath my feet.

That crevasse would not have been noticed by any of the Muskeg or International tractors but one crevasse we failed to find with the dogs was indeed noticed by a tractor. It was the start of a tractor reconnaissance and we were almost safely through the hinge zone when Dad Etchells our chief driver and mechanic, as well as one of the most experienced fids at Halley, stopped his vehicle to check a suspect bit of ground ahead. Chris Sykes the other driver mechanic, was in the second vehicle and as the probing and checking was taking some time, he switched off his engine. Dad returned and drove off; Chris switched on his engine. Now when a large powerful engine starts up, it shudders and vibrates before settling down. Chris's engine shuddered and vibrated and the whole vehicle settled… in a crevasse directly under him.

The whole situation could have been disastrous but Dad in his wisdom had equipped the tractors with crash frames. These frames, made of scaffolding and welded to the tractor chassis, were an attempt to prevent the type of occurrence that was uppermost in Dad's mind when he fitted them.

In 1965 Jeremy Bailey, John Wilson, Dai Wild and Ian Ross were working in the Tottanfjella. Their route from the base camp had been round a quite large bend. On the way back they had taken the short cut and hit a large hidden crevasse. Ian had been riding alone on a towed sledge and looking back the way they had come. Suddenly the sledge stopped, he turned to inquire the reason but there was no tractor, just a large hole where it should have been. It had broken its tow bracket and fallen in backwards to a considerable depth, crushing the cab and Ian's three companions in the narrowing hole.

Dad's crash frame most definitely did save Chris and his tractor for it too tried to drop in backwards, but as it tipped, it jack-knifed vertically with the sledge behind and the crash frame jammed against the loaded tanker sledge. For Chris it must have been, and continued for some minutes to be a harrowing incident. For we observers, it happened so quickly and the locking of tractor and sledge so obviously secure, that we laughed. Chris's vain shouts of help were met with, "Just hold on while I get my camera!"

The possibility of "keg swallowers" was always a concern, especially with the much heavier International tractors for it was doubtful that anything could save such a monster if it decided to take a vertical ride. One solution in terms of lives if not tractor was the fitting of remote controls. Track laying vehicles have no steering wheel, just a couple of levers. Pull the right lever to turn right, the left for left. Also like all tractors, they have a "sticky" throttle, that is an accelerator that can be set at the desired engine revs. All that was needed were four ropes fed out through a port in the back of the cab. Two controlled the turn levers, the other two (one through a pulley) could activate the throttle if necessary. It worked very well but sitting, unprotected, on a hard sledge for several hours was not pleasant. Also, being behind the tractor cab we could not see the detail of the ground immediately in front. Careful probing on foot and careful driving from the cab was more efficient but even so, accidents could happen.

In 1969 one of the International tractors did drop through a Bob Pi crevasse. Fortunately it dropped horizontally and it jammed only a few metres down. The driver escaped unhurt but the tractor was regarded as lost. Lost that is until 1972 when Bruce Blackwell (diesel mechanic), planned, and with the help of Ian Bury, Gordon Ramage and David Fletcher, successfully recovered the machine. After a dust down and battery change the tractor was started and driven back to base!

• • •

Dog teams may be lighter than tractors but they can still drop through hidden holes, and as the Bob Pi slope, down which we sledged, gave way to the flatter ground of the hinge zone our caution increased. Apart from two very large, very obvious and easily avoided crevasses the terrain looked relatively innocuous but we knew it contained many nasty secrets, some known, some not. We took turns to ski ahead, checking and probing, checking and probing before signalling the teams to follow. Fortunately there seemed to have been little change since our traverse of four months previous. The intricate line was clearly flagged and our logbook details tallied with the flag line. With growing and justified confidence we gradually worked our way through the crossing.

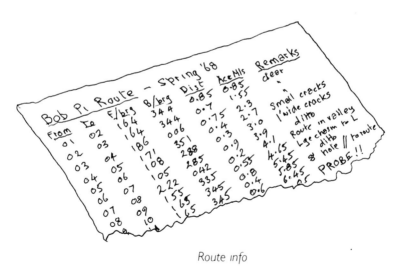

Route info

A page torn from my Bob Pi recce log book
showing the "legs" from flag to flag.

17 Blizzard

Before leaving England I had what I presume were anxiety dreams. I had really no idea what to expect except the polar scenery was supposed to be breathtaking. I knew of Scott, of Mawson, of Shackleton but that was not too reassuring: Scott had died along with four of his colleagues, Mawson had lost his two sledging partners and all but died himself on a long lonely haul back to his base, Shackleton had lost his ship and, with his entire crew, had suffered many months of harsh privation before effecting their own rescue. From my mountaineering experience I knew of several top flight mountaineers who had either died from hypothermia or who had lost fingers, toes, whole limbs to frostbite in the equivalent polar temperatures of high altitude climbing. And then there were the stories of glacier travellers falling into crevasses. It didn't auger too well.

I had no truly relevant personal experience on which my dreams could be based so they were a confusion of strange doubt and unease permeating ordinary dream situations.

When I returned from the South I had more anxiety dreams but this time they had a focus and it was always the same. I am walking away from a polar base towards a snow dome. It is my job to check it out. When I get to the top I notice a crevasse and stop to probe it. The fragile bridge instantly drops away to reveal not just a vertical drop to infinity but one in which the crevasse walls rapidly curl under. I am standing on an overhang. I retreat but find another hole has opened up behind me with the same overhangs. The same happens to left and right. I am now standing on a tall slender mushroom of

John Gallsworthy, Nick Mathys and the Mobsters

The Theron Mountains and my sledge bag

Mike Skidmore and Peter Noble beside "Llareggub Cairn"
at Pt Touché just over 80°S - Jan 1968

"Four tractors and twelve sledges with a twenty nine ton load"

International Harvester ready for the field

Climbing the Bob Pi Slope from the ice shelf

Crossing the high plateau

About 1/10th of the parhelic display on the high plateau

Depot Dad established at Mt Shelleen (later called Lundstrøm Knoll)

The "Overland Shacks" team in the Eastern Shackletons
Alan Etchells, Peter Noble, John Carter, Stuart MacQuarrie, John Gallsworthy, Norris Riley

A summit of the Eastern Shackleton Range

In the Shackletons

Snow hills of the Eastern Shackletons (Pioneer Escarpment) from Mt Shelleen.
The tracks lead to the buttress from which the jade green "Adventurine" was taken.

Day's end

snow and as I watch more and more snow bridges collapse until I am looking down into a total void. The whole snow dome is hollow and is now just a surface net of narrow unsupported bridges. The entire structure should disintegrate but it never does for I wake up.

Although we searched for crevasses, probed and crossed them, even camped between ice falls, at no time during our travels did I experience overhangs or closely interlinked crevasses. At no time did I have any real fear of falling into one, indeed I descended one out of interest and collected several beautiful palm sized, six sided, plate crystals that chimed like wine glasses. But when on or near ice falls and particularly at night as we lay in our sleeping bags, we often heard the ice banging and cracking in the depths like Tolkein's drums in the deeps of Moria. But why the belated anxiety? Only after all my crossings of the Bob Pi did I hear the stories of disaster and near disaster on that twenty mile run of Russian roulette.

Gordon Mallinson and Gordon Bowra were on their way home from the Tottan Range in 1964 when they dropped their entire dog team down a Bob Pi crevasse. Fortunately the two Gordons plus their sledge did not follow the dogs, and even though some of the dogs fell out of their harnesses, all nine were recovered little the worse for their unseemly descent into the void. Scarcely had they regrouped however when the huskies safely crossed an unseen bridge but the Gordons and their sledge broke through. Their companion sledge of Sam Samuel and Dick Worsfold were able to extricate the pair from their cavernous predicament, again little the worse from their three hour entombment.

Sadly, and long after I had returned to England, a full dog team again dropped down a hole but on that occasion there was no happy ending for the dogs. There were and would be enough crevasse stories to cause my subsequent anxiety dreams, but strangely absent from my adventuring slumbers are any dreams with high winds.

• • •

As Mike and I drove the Hairybreeks from flag to flag through the Bob Pi Crossing I hoped we would not meet any difficulties to cause us delay. I anticipated problems at the "keg swallower" , the hole that had taken a liking to Chris Sykes' Muskeg, but we made an easy detour. I also expected possible delays in an area known as "Drum Valley" as it was known to have more rapid snow accumulation than elsewhere - would the route markings still be visible? As we swung left into the valley all was well, the route ahead was clearly flagged and the surface looked good. The Bob Pi seemed in benevolent mood. I wasn't yet to know it but the Crossing would be considerably less hospitable the next time, but it would not be the crevasses that showed hostility.

That next time was the September following our return from the Shackletons reconnaissance, when three dog teams and six men set out to check the crossing for the new season. This season was to be somewhat different for the heavy International Harvester tractors would be on expedition for the first time, and they would have to cross the Bob Pi. We couldn't afford to make a mistake as we knew we wouldn't pull an International out as easily as the 'keg.

Many of the Shackletons dogs were by then retired necessitating the formation of new teams so I had assembled a modest crew that contained four of my old team. I named them the "Treacleminers" after the mythical industry of my home town. (My brother and I had also formed a skiffle group in our early teens under the same name!). My new partner was Norris Riley (GA). Harry Wiggans (GA) teamed up with Bill Laidlaw (meteorologist) to run another new team but retained an existing team name: the "Beatles". Mike Skidmore worked with his fellow geologist and later base commander, Peter Clarkson and ran another new team: the "Hobbits". Although it was Bill's second year he was not a field man so his experience behind dogs was little more than that of Norris, Harry or Rocky who were all starting their first season. It was to be a baptism of fire, though the metaphor is perhaps inappropriately warm.

Moderately good progress was made in very cold conditions and minus forty degrees was recorded one day when we all suffered frequent cold nip. Technically this is frostbite but it strikes suddenly, and is very localised on exposed flesh, especially the cheeks and ears. Although I always seemed aware of its onset, since it felt like being flicked with an elastic band, some of the others felt nothing and it was essential to keep glancing at one's partner's face to see if there were any white spots appearing where the blood no longer flowed. The cure was simple and quick. A gloved hand (fortunately not necessary to remove the glove) applied to the face and a gentle massage always worked. Some years later I was publicly ridiculed by an experienced mountain instructor when I recommended massaging early frostbite - it ain't what the book says!

Harry did cause me some concern as his hands were going numb, but by chance we had to stop early that day to tend a dog injury and Harry also recovered fully.

The following day we made an easy run to the start of the Bob Pi and by the end of the third day, half of the Bob Pi was satisfactorily checked and reflagged... but then the wind started to increase. Thus far it had been a fairly constant 15 mph, the speed at which progress normally stops as the snow is lifted into spindrift and one cannot see the surface. This is often acceptable on the crevasse free plateau but obviously not in the Bob Pi, strangely however, on this occasion no significant spindrift had developed and work had continued, despite the unpleasantly frostbiting wind.   As it increased beyond workable limits we pitched the tents close to Drum Valley which dramatically sported a major crevasse down either side of the campsite.

Over the next four days a storm raged, buffeting the tents, drifting over the dogs, half burying the sledges. We lay there wondering when, then if, it would end. We had a shovel and a saw and perhaps there was some sense in digging an emergency snow hole in case the tent should take off or disintegrate, but the constant buffeting seemed to numb the brain, or maybe I just never thought of it for "snow-holing" was a concept still unknown to me. It would be another three years before I dug and slept in my first snow hole in the Cairngorms of Scotland. Whatever the reason for inactivity we would just think we were getting used to the onslaught when when a sudden heavier gust would stagger the tent and I for one would break out in a cold sweat. Conversation was desultory: I don't think anyone wanted to voice his real thoughts.

By noon on the fifth day the wind died and we crawled outside. There were large drifts where none had been before. The dogs and the sledges had to be dug out but we left the tents erected as there was route checking to be done close by. The calm was short lived and reflagging was curtailed by late afternoon as the wind rose again. What we had experienced before paled now by comparison. Fifty, sixty, seventy miles an hour, perhaps more. Ninety mph was recorded at Halley. The storm was relentless, implacable, thunderous and frightening.

All I can remember of the next four days was rigging a safety line between all the tents and recommending that we all stay fully clothed and keep all equipment stowed in our large personal bags or the utility boxes until it was needed, and that it should be restowed immediately after use. The less we lost if a tent blew away, the better our chances of survival.

You think you can get used to anything, the roll of a ship, the noise of living near an airport or beside a motorway, but you don't get used to the sudden gusts that punctuate a major storm when camped on polar ice, and miles from help or security. Every single blast shocks one's senses and jangles one's nerves; muscles are tensed repeatedly, the fight-or-flight mechanism kicking in at every heavy battering. Sleep comes fitfully with exhaustion, both mental and physical.

On the tenth day after setting up Camp Storm, the sky cleared and the wind died. It was quiet, so quiet we could once more hear the occasional banging of the ice hinge deep below. We gazed about, relieved, bemused, benumbed: we were now camped in three distinct valleys, one for each tent, for large drifts had built up around us with a wind scoop downwind of every tent. I tried to salvage something of the reconnaissance and sent Harry and Norris ahead with a strengthened dog team to test the going but they were soon floundering in deep snow and unable to detect crevasses. Very sensibly they turned back. My report of the time is very matter of fact in that we completed what we could of the reconnaissance - though much was lost under the new snow - and sledged home. It does not mention my frustration nor my relief.

• • •

Heading home from the Shackleton recce with Mike, Nick and Golly it was perhaps fortunate that we knew nothing of that future trip as the Hairybreeks and Mobsters descended Drum Valley, negotiated the twisting route out of the crossing and headed for the safety of the crevasse free ice shelf, but our progress was temporarily and pleasantly interrupted.

At the exit of the Bob Pi was a tent, a sledge, glaciologists Paul Coslett and Andrew Wager plus coffee and cake.

As we supped, munched and chatted, I found myself gazing at their bright yellow Skidoo, a motor toboggan that carried two people and would pull a useful sledge load of camping gear and supplies. I glanced at my nine loveable huskies, curled up, resting and then back at the inanimate cold Skidoo. I wouldn't have swapped, but little did I realise I was looking at the past and the future.

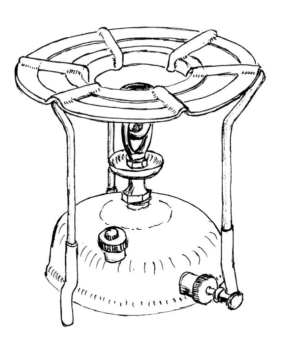

The two pint "Primus" or "Optimus" paraffin stove

18 The Beginning of the End

As a very young boy I used to stand on a railway bridge to watch the steam trains pass through our local station. It was all very exciting, especially when the train steamed under my bridge and enveloped me in clouds of smoke, but more exciting was when the new train arrived. It had two very new carriages and no engine, and it pulled out of the station with the roar of a heavy lorry. No billowing smoke, no hissing steam, not even a whistle, just a column of exhaust and a two tone horn. I had just seen my first diesel. It was an oddity, something unique, but little did I realise that within a few weeks I would never again see a steam train in service. Less did I realise, and nor would I have believed, that within a decade there would be a housing estate where the obviously essential railway station then stood.

I was a slow learner about progress for when more new houses replaced the old blacksmith shop, when the market place was demolished for a bus station, when the town hall was modernised, it was the new that I photographed with my first camera. I somehow regarded the old as permanent and the new as strange and temporary, in need of recording. I suspect I somehow believed that the old buildings would return when the novelty of development had worn off!

Yes I was a slow learner and I hadn't improved when I arrived at Halley. There I encountered the strange and quite unreliable Eliason motor toboggan. I suppose in my mind I equated it with the failed motorised transport attempts of Scott. I also equated it with the prototype electric tooth brushes which we were given to test. A report would be written, the machines sent home for examination and we would get back to dogs and hand driven toothbrushes.

My perception was strengthened with each breakdown of the Eliason - known on base as the Elsan for various deducible reasons. My only direct contact with it was to rescue it and its cargo sledges during my own tractor expedition when our mechanics effected field repairs. Nevertheless it did keep going (with help) for several years.

Originally there had been two Eliasons, "Clem" and "Sadie" sent down for the 1963 field season and named to honour Ray "Clem" Clements and his wife who lived in Port Stanley. Clem was in charge of supplies at our Falkland Islands office and both he and Sadie were very welcoming and hospitable to passing fids. Unfortunately the Eliasons themselves did not honour the couple, and the first excursion report was quite damning, claiming inadequate power, too many breakages and needing Muskeg support. They were in fact too highly geared which accounted for their lack of power at the low speeds required by the heavy loads and difficult terrain. The Eliason had obviously been designed as a snow motorbike, not the mini tractor that was needed. By 1967 our Sadie had been cannibalised to keep her metallic partner operational. Noting the number of times Clem broke down during my first year at Halley Bay I felt quite certain that these motor toboggans were a passing phase... even when two, more modern devices called Skidoos were delivered.

The new machines soon acquired the names "Kathleen" and "Mol" after the wives of their two regular drivers Big Al Smith and Jo Porter (GA) but it took a full overhaul and a total repaint in bright yellow for Clem to earn feminine distinction as "Daffodil".

The tradition of naming various forms of transport was quite general and even spread to the dog sledges with Nick

Mathys - he who would recite Kipling's "If" and mean it - titling his sledge "Empire Builder". In later years sledge names and their call signs became less romantic by using the Greek alphabet. Were fids becoming boring and unimaginative?

Perhaps imagination comes in cycles for there is no record of the first motorised vehicle being named. That was a Ferguson farm tractor who's only modification for Antarctic work was the addition of tracks connecting the front and back wheels. No heater, not even a cab to shelter the driver from the wind. However, although Sir Edmund Hilary had successfully met Vivian Fuchs at the South Pole using Fergusons, the Halley machine was not an expedition vehicle, being restricted to operations around the base.

The Ferguson was upgraded to a Bombardier Muskeg in 1960 and six found their way to Halley during the next five years. Two were briefly named "Stancombe" and "Wills" possibly after Janet Stancombe Wills, one of Ernest Shackleton's sponsors, though it is more likely they were named after the eponymous glacier which no doubt they were expected to traverse and which itself *was* named for Sir Ernest's sponsor. Regardless, all 'kegs became generally known by their number, one to six. By contrast the first two International tractors, introduced in 1966, were named in England before dispatch. The manager of the Leeds company that modified the machines for polar work named them after the two BAS representatives (ex-Halley men) with whom he liaised: "Peter" Blakeley and "Paul" Whiteman. Inevitably when a third machine was ordered it was immediately christened "Mary", thus completing the very popular 1960s folk group.

I didn't have a name for my own sledge other than my call sign of "Ake" but the dog teams were always named. This was in fact a rather strange concept since the composition of each team varied as dogs were regularly swapped about. For two men to say they ran with the same team at different times had in fact little reference to any particular group of dogs. Nevertheless, teams were formed and titled. The first two Halley teams to run, in 1961, were the Hairybreeks and the Second Team though whether "second team" is a name or a simple reference is unclear from sledging reports. Later came the Mobsters ('63), Beatles ('65), Hobbits ('67), Treacleminers ('68), Muckletrappers ('70) and Femlins ('72) though the last three were rather short lived.

It seemed to me that though the composition of the teams changed, dog travel itself was permanent, unthreatened by those modern, noisy, unreliable motor toboggans, for even Kathleen and Mol kept breaking down. How could those lumps of machinery that kept having to be rescued compete with our stock of around sixty enthusiastic dogs that seemed willing, nay eager, to run anywhere, anytime.

There was also the theory that a dog team in crevassed country was by far the safest means of travel, a theory I agreed with throughout my stay at Halley but then, I was a doggyman and refused to accept any alternative, much less countenance the demise of my dogs.

The writing would soon be on the wall however, or more particularly at the bottom of a crevasse, for in 1972, four years after my leaving Halley there was a serious accident that made me and BAS reappraise our respective ideas.

Two teams were being driven through the Hinge Zone, checking the "Wright Line" a new crossing discovered by Graham Wright and party in 1970. Jack Donaldson and Toby Stoneham driving the Hobbits encountered a hidden crevasse. The dogs were trotting obliquely across its bridge oblivious to the depths below when the sledge punctured the surface and lurched sideways. Toby who was sitting on the sledge, rolled safely off, just before it dropped through into the void. The weight was too much for the dogs and the entire team was pulled backwards, down into their cold blue grave.

Jack and Toby were left on the surface, lucky not only to be alive but to have another team close behind since every bit of their survival gear was down the crevasse, and the crevasse was deep, very deep. Dave Fletcher (GA) descended some distance on a rope but they had insufficient resources to reach the dogs or sledge far below. There was nothing for it but to return to base.

The subsequent salvage party found the team and sledge 55 metres down. Inevitably all the dogs were dead and they included four of my old Shackletons' team, Changi (who had become an excellent leader), Luqa, Wensen and Esk. Strange how learning and writing of the death of "my" dogs, though now remote in place and time, brings a tightening to the throat.

The Environmental Protocol of the Antarctic Treaty required that all dogs be removed from Antarctica by 1994. The husky population at Halley at the time of the 1972 accident had already been downsized from over sixty at its peak in 1968 to a modest thirty five, but perhaps it was the Hobbits' tragedy that hammered the final, if premature nail in the coffin of serious dog travel. Only three further dog expeditions would be undertaken before the entire Halley stock of huskies would be rescheduled, leaving just two animals on base as pets.

Shem, the only survivor of my original team, along with seventeen other dogs and bitches, would be transferred to the "Banana Belt" (as the Halley men referred to the more northerly bases on the Antarctic Peninsula).

The remaining fifteen animals were to be culled - the polite spelling of killed.

Unrealised by me in 1967/68 as I travelled and played with my dogs, the motor toboggans were proving their potential, even their worth. Glaciologists Bob Thomas, Paul Coslett and Andrew Wager (spanning all my time at Halley) became adepts at keeping the mechanical beasts running, and travelled many hundreds of miles on their numerous glaciological surveys around the ice shelf and even venturing onto the inland ice through the hinge zone. There were two major advantages of Skidoos, which we doggymen would find difficult to accept. Firstly, assuming reliability, they were more efficient. Skidoos could pull a full load without the need of rest stops every fifty minutes; and they travelled at three to four times the speed of dogs. A four or five day expedition with dogs was a simple day out with a Skidoo; a month with dogs required a prior Muskeg trip to lay food depots, whereas a Skidoo towed all it needed for the mere week that would cover the equivalent ground!

The Hobbit accident, the Mallinson and Bowra incidents, the very close shave of Wornham and Swift plus a few other near misses, were suggesting that reconnaissance work with dogs was not necessarily the safest method as we had been led to believe. Whatever the transport, in crevassed country everyone had to probe carefully ahead. Failure to do so could spell disaster. Perhaps this knowledge plus the awareness that a man on a Skidoo is considerable more vulnerable than a man behind a dog team, made the Skidoo drivers more thorough in their probing. Certainly, in my experience, no Skidoo ever dropped down any crevasse. The dog sledge record is not so good.

• • •

There were however no such analytical or pessimistic thoughts in my mind as we clattered and creaked homeward bound from that lonely cairn near the Shackleton Mountains across the last few miles of ice shelf to Halley Bay. The mountains, the Slessor Glacier, the high plateau, the Bob Pi crossing, the whole six hundred miles were now behind us. Ahead the radio aerials, the radar shack with its large dish aerial, the meteorological balloon launching shed, a few other surface structures and, most importantly for us, the access shafts to our home, itself now and forever buried below the snow surface.

There would be a brief, somewhat disappointing, heroes welcome. There would be a good meal, a little alcohol, old friends to greet, new fidlets to meet... but strangely few stories to relate: no one seemed particularly interested! Maybe there was a modicum of resentment in that folks left on base had had to take on our chores whilst we had all the fun, but perhaps it was more the case that we had been doing our job and they were doing theirs... and I don't recall my asking anyone how they had got on over the summer!

The whole reconnaissance from Halley to the furthest south (including false hopes down dead ends) plus the return trip covered some 1,400 miles of which I dog-sledged 984, the rest being as a tractor driver or passenger. Though this did not compare with the 1,560 miles sledged by Geoff Lovegrove and Patrick "Tony" Haynes two years earlier in the Heimfrontfjella, it nevertheless felt a fair achievement.

True we had failed to reach rock but we all, Nick, Golly, Mike and I, felt quite pleased. There had been no mishaps; and despite the rejection of our proposed route for next year, we felt we had effectively "proved" it a feasibility.

The six hundred mile run home had suffered its Mobster frustrations and bad weather delays but we had made it in respectable time. A telegram was sent to Colin Wornham and all the others, now back in England, who had launched us on our wonderful adventure:

"Six hundred miles? A piece of yellow ice!"

19   You Oughta See 'em From My Side

The 1968 midwinter film had been carefully hidden until the appropriate date by our base commander, so it was with the special pleasure of both surprise and genuine enjoyment that we watched the classic western spoof "Cat Ballou". The lovely and extremely shapely Jane Fonda (especially in that tight red dress) plays the eponymous school ma'am turned train robber but the quote of the film is by her drunken hired gun slinger "Kid Shelleen" (Lee Marvin). Shelleen *and* his horse are both leaning against a wall and both looking very much the worse for drink. "Kid," exclaims his young apprentice, "look at your eyes". "What's wrong with my eyes?" growls Shelleen. "Well they're red, bloodshot," which earns the much quoted retort "You oughta see 'em from my side".

By the end of that winter at Halley Bay we were virtually word perfect on the entire sound track but it was many years later that I realised I had never applied Shelleen's observation to my perception of Halley. I had never attempted to see Halley from the point of view of the more or less base bound boys. Never from their side.

Running field expeditions was the purpose of being in Antarctica for several of us at Halley but this was not the case for the majority: the scientists, technicians and support staff, whose work was focused on Halley itself. Our long expeditions to remote mountains were important in expanding geographical and geological understanding of Antarctica but for the stay-at-homes they were an adjunct to normal life and work. Regrettably those of us who journeyed out from the base, even on short trips, rarely if ever considered the effect our absence had on those left to mind the shop. Detailed duty rostas calculated for the full complement of men had to be rescheduled for a reduced team which meant their chores were more frequent. Added to this there was always a touch of glamour in field men returning triumphantly from a long expedition, glamour which inevitably by-passed, and possibly annoyed, those doing the daily essentials of maintaining the base and making meteorological and other atmospheric observations. I never thanked those guys for making my work feasible - I do so now most sincerely if somewhat belatedly.

We field men thought we had it tough when sledging and camping in the early 'spring' or late 'autumn' but the static scientists and others had their unpleasant times too. In the winter months when we GAs and tractor men might be ensconced in a nice warm garage or workshop preparing for another season, or when we could schedule outside work to avoid the worst weather, the meteorologists and geophysicists would be obliged to brave the very conditions we chose to avoid. Regardless of blizzard, winter dark or plummeting temperatures they would venture forth to undertake their routine daily measurements. There was also the sobering realisation for us that whereas our field trips were notionally interesting and might earn our field scientists an MSc or two, their static work was invaluable. The meteorological observations (which earned no university degree) were of specific use to the southern continents, especially South Africa and more importantly in assisting understanding on how global weather works. I sometimes wonder if the met office scientists in warmer climes who analysed and played with Halley data ever thought of the guys who on a pitch black winter day with temperatures down to minus fifty tried to read the various thermometers, barometers and hygrometers in the Stevenson Screen. The geophysicists, Jim Jamieson and Jim Chalmers during my Halley stint, occasionally had it even harder for to ensure that their delicate instruments were unsullied by vibrations from the base, from tractors or even from straying pedestrians they had been allocated a circle of virgin snow, half a mile in diameter in the centre of which was their tiny hut that housed the precious instruments. No one was allowed near the place except a geophysicist at specific times. If that specific time coincided with a blizzard it was a cold, hazardous and lonely walk to that little hut.

Generally, as to scientific observations, if it could be seen or experienced it was examined and measured and sometimes it was measured when it could be neither seen nor experienced. It was at Halley that measurements of the ionosphere led to the discovery of the hole in the world's defences against harmful radiation. Halley also provided a singularly isolated community that could not be "polluted" by outside influences, hence we could be and were experimented upon by doctors and physiologists such as Doc John with his infuriating breathing apparatus and also his successor Doc Murray Roberts who, in cahoots with John Fry (physiologist) substituted our normal sugar with a glucose based substitute that didn't dissolve very well in tea. Sugar was confiscated (except for the lucky control group) and even the chocolate ration was substituted with a new not so pleasant sugar free variety. Experimentation was everywhere. Walk into a scientists office and apart from the inevitable mug of coffee and the clack of typewriter as reports were written up, there might be wires and radio valves and other paraphernalia strewn around as the standard equipment supplied was sometimes unsuitable and in need of modification but more usually new equipment was required that had to be designed and built from scratch.

The 2006 reunion at Cambridge (the reunion that kick started this book) demonstrated the vast changes since the 1960s and led to much good natured grumbling, especially when we were video linked to Halley and spoke directly in real time to the people on base: "Don't know how lucky they are with all those mod cons", "daily e-mails! we had to make do with fifty words a month by teleprinter and letters once a year" and "committed to two years we were, now they just fly in for a month or two's jolly" and then the inevitable but true "not like that in my day". And so it went on but I detected and felt a certain pride in the privations we had experienced and the resourcefulness on which we flourished.

Even by the then current standards we were somewhat archaically equipped as most of our basic kit had not changed since the 1940s or even earlier. While ordinary British climbers (not just Himalayan expeditions) were feeling snug in down filled jackets we were still wearing heavy kapok. My testing of a pair of double mountaineering boots was a breakthrough though they had been around in mountaineering circles for several years, but the one new and very welcome item under test was a track suit made of artificial fleece, the forerunner of modern fleece clothing. I smuggled my own test suit back to the UK and used it for over thirty years to great benefit from its comfort and warmth in winter mountaineering, skiing and caving.

Warmth inside the base at Halley was however in rather limited supply. We possessed two Rolls Royce generators that were run sequentially for the purposes of servicing and back up, and each one was designed to give adequate power for lighting, electrical equipment and heating. Unfortunately someone had forgotten to tell the contractor that the machines would be fuelled on the ubiquitous Avtur. Avtur apparently needs special fuel injection jets that are somewhat different to the standard diesel jets we received, consequently those luxury promising RR power supplies did not produce the anticipated "spirit of ecstasy" rather one of mild chill. This affected us little in our daily work and it certainly ensured the bunk rooms were maintained at a healthy temperature, but stripping off for the weekly shower could be a minor challenge. Perhaps socially more important, the spacious lounge was scarcely useable except when filled by a full complement of heat generating fids, though whether the heat was bodies or mere hot air is a moot point. Nevertheless the weekly assemblies in the lounge were great fun. It was a time to relax, chat to lads one hadn't seen much of during the week (easily done on a base with several large huts), watch the Saturday film for the fourth, fifth or tenth time and peruse the "Pengwinge" our laboriously typed monthly magazine to which several of us contributed articles, jokes, puzzles, whatever came to mind.

There was an authentic looking bar complete with beer pumps, but the assembly beneath the bar was anything but authentic for there were no actual pumps, no pipe work and no barrels; all beer supplied by BAS was in cans and this was strictly rationed to two cans per person per week which was unlikely to cause overt drunken behaviour. Even Johnny Carter's special consignment would scarcely produce an alcoholic reverie (unless he were to consume a month's supply in one night!). Shorts were in similar limited supply but, like Johnny, several people had enhanced their personal allocation by importing gin and whisky from Port Stanley. G&T was the regular if unlikely tipple for private and guest consumption in the "Black Gang" office.

There were no cliques as such at Halley but there developed natural interest or affinity groups. One could drift from one to another and there was no question or criticism, and certainly no lack of welcome, but inevitably various groups did coalesce. These seemed to focus, perhaps understandably, not just on jobs but also on the four huts that were the focus of those jobs. In the furthest end of the furthest hut, far from the communal rooms, was the "met" office, and being the largest office with the largest number of residents, the scientists from adjacent offices congregated there, complete with the two cats Kista, who was smuggled aboard the supply ship "Kista Dan" in 1961 and brought to Halley, and Kosmo, similarly smuggled, from Port Stanley and named (if misspelled) after Sir Cosmo Haskard the then Governor of the Falkland Islands. The thought of Kosmo the cat's namesake brings back embarrassing memories.

Possibly because there was little diplomatic activity in Britain's forgotten remnant of empire, for this was pre-Falklands War, there were few opportunities for Sir Cosmo and his lady wife to entertain foreign dignitaries, consequently the arrival of fifty government employees aboard the Royal Research Ship "John Biscoe" was a good excuse to redress the balance. The fact that we were lowly fids made no difference, we were royally entertained as was every ship load of fids that headed south. Upon docking at Port Stanley an invitation to a reception at "The Residence" had been received and we all smartened up into clean shirts, suits and ties. Remembering the polite protocol of arriving a little late I was one of the last to turn up at the bun fight and noticed with interest that a couple of Biscoe lads had commandeered the bar and were serving the drinks. I should have been on my guard. Not being a serious drinker and not knowing how long the reception might last I resolved to start quietly with something to dilute any later intake of alcohol as I didn't want to commit any social faux pas. I asked for a still orange with a dash of lime but did not notice what went into my glass because my eye was caught by an attractive young lady whose boldly presented bosom and flirtatious glance suggested that she too might regularly entertain passing fids. A nearby local man had a very different expression that distinctly warned me and everyone else off his property so I drained my glass, moved away and grazed on the many plates of tempting sandwiches, cakes and other goodies. In due course, with a fresh orange and lime in my hand, I was introduced to Lady Haskard and held her in animated conversation, impressing her with my erudition, my witty remarks and my increasing inebriation. I learned later that my orange and lime had been diluted not with water but neat vodka! Lady Haskard was the perfect hostess and politely listened (or expertly pretended to) as I became more and more incoherent. Too late, something sluggishly clicked in my grey matter and I made an apologetic exit. I distinctly recall performing perfect cartwheels down the high street and ending with a flawless handstand on the very end of the pier - it seems I was far more in control upside down than on my feet!

Back amongst the Halley reception venues there was also a general gathering place in the kitchen that attracted the field scientists, particularly the glaciologists whose own office was in the same hut, plus the on duty skivvies or "gash 'ands" whose job it was that day to clean the public rooms and corridors, get rid of accumulated rubbish, fill the melt tanks and generally help the cooks. This meeting place was decidedly the warmest spot on base and many a painful pile was developed through sitting on the Aga cooker. Across the tunnel beyond the lounge was the "radio shack", another conveniently large room that offered hospitality and refuge from "gash" duties and other urgent work. Its only drawback was its immediate proximity to the base commander's office. The fourth retreat was a tiny office in the corner of the garage - the home of the "Black Gang" the dirty hand brigade of diesel and tractor mechanics, electricians, carpenters and other itinerant maintenance personnel. In keeping with garages world wide the walls were tastefully if tantalisingly decorated with delicious ladies, most being minimally dressed, the rest were less well covered. Oddly doggymen did not have a group home (except on expedition) so we tended to drift or attach ourselves to other gangs - especially the Black Gang for some reason.

"Smoko" was however the twice daily gathering of the

full base complement in the dining room for elevenses and three thirties. Tea, coffee and steaming fresh bread rolls would be served in vast quantity in the mornings, cakes in the afternoons, thus completely ruining appetites for the midday and evening meals. Smoko was also the time for notices and whole team discussions. Many a smoko would be punctuated with a mild somewhat embarrassed cough from the base commander followed by, "Whilst you're all here..." and this would start some debate or the imparting of some information. Inevitably after several weeks we would hear the cough, see the BC stand up, and some other voice (or several) would recite the expected words to loud guffaws and the BC's tolerant amusement.

A much anticipated *whilst-you're-all-here* was the announcement of Midwinter celebrations. The 21st of June marked the turning point of our dark months and after fifty days of continuous midnight outside, some merriment and celebration was needed. The format was simple: a sumptuous meal, a better than normal allocation of drink, a new film, perhaps some in-house entertainment such as the staged review we put on in my first year, and two days to recover. The catering was indeed magnificent, topped in that same first year by a beautifully sculpted cake in the shape of Antarctica with the BAS coat of arms in bas(!) relief in the centre; a work of art by our gifted and ever resourceful cooks. There was also a very heart warming surprise in store that first midwinter for after the meal the base commander, who had quietly absented himself, returned in Santa Claus role, insofar as he had a large beard (his own) and a large sack on his back.

"I have a few presents to give out from folks back home," he announced; and if the others were like me then we all thought *a few* meant "to a few people but excluding me!" More and more presents were produced until everyone had some gift from parents or wife. Commander Ricky had thoughtfully contacted our close relations before we sailed south and unknown by us our presents had accompanied us on the voyage south.

That midwinter the special film was the heist spoof "Topkapi" and was much enjoyed but it was the following midwinter that we met (or rather wish we could have met) "Cat Ballou" (especially in that tight red dress). Impressed though we all were, the lads had the last word for as we sat down to dine, in walked three hairy legged waitresses dressed as Bunny Girls - complete with bunny tails, bunny ears, bunny bathing costumes, braces and beards!

There was hilarious laughter and many a groping hand. "Looks like your boobs are slipping," I commented to one who shall remain nameless.

"You should see 'em from my side," he (she) retorted.

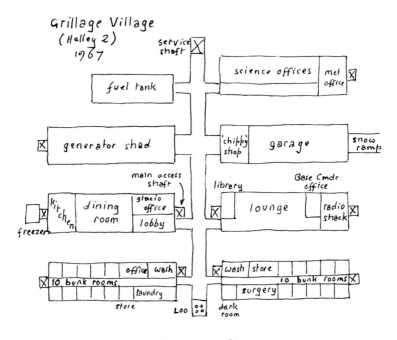

Grillage Village Plan

20 Nansen House

One assumes that Fridjof Nansen did design the Nansen dog sledge that bears his name but perhaps he modified or simply popularised a well established vehicle. Whoever did design it merits some award, for the concept and construction is as excellent as it is simple. Essentially the "Nansen" is an over sized kiddie's sledge with wide ski runners instead of the usual narrow steel ones and a handlebar frame at the back. The beauty of the construction was the choice of ash for the timber, being strong, light and flexible, also the total lack of glue and the avoidance of screws as much as possible. The four metre long runners were connected by five "bridges" that were tenoned into the runners and secured with rawhide thonging. The longitudinal spars or stringers were then lashed to the bridges with "codline", a robust string that was then doped to tighten the lashing. A long flexible board with spikes in one end was similarly lashed lengthways under the bridges and formed a brake that could be stood on to drive the spikes into the ice. It didn't very work well in soft snow, but then, neither did the dogs! The handlebar frame was held on with u-bolted fish plates and tensioned into rigidity with cross wires and bottle screws. And when assembled the whole sledge was linseed oiled to preserve the virtue of the timber. I had become more than familiar with the construction, I knew every detail in detail. The amounts of cord and rawhide for the lashings, the number of bolts, the lengths and diameters of the various ropes for standing and running rigging, centre traces, side traces, special fittings...

In the winter of '67, my first winter, a team of we doggymen had stripped and rebuilt fourteen Nansen's. I suspect that only a few had needed such a complete rebuild as most of the lashings looked in excellent condition but it seemed a sort of tradition to totally refurbish all field gear. There was however a weakness in the design of the bridges. They were constructed of two pillars and a cross piece with a diagonal metal brace at each angle to prevent the whole bridge from collapsing. This brace was lashed to the timbers with iron wire that then had solder run all over it to form a solid piece of metal, but as it was the only rigid component on a flexible sledge it remained a weakness, and bridges occasionally broke, necessitating tedious repairs.

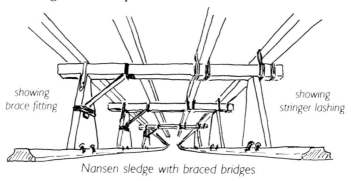

showing
brace fitting

showing
stringer lashing

Nansen sledge with braced bridges

The "mark 2" sledge that I fortunately inherited from Colin Wornham solved this problem in having the bridges made of laminated timber, steamed and glued into the required bridge shape. No joints, no braces, no soldered wire. There was another advantage: the bends from horizontal to vertical could not be a sharp angle as in the old design, and this pushed the runners further apart making the sledge significantly more stable. We did not appreciate this until we realised that other sledges occasionally capsized - ours never did.

The work on the sledges had been hard but good fun and we became adepts at rope splicing, whippings, lashings and forming *turk's head* knots.

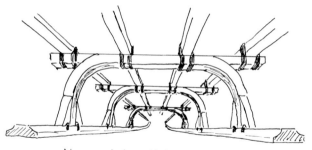
Nansen sledge with laminated bridges

During my first year when Colin was in charge of we GAs, we were fortunate in having the use of a newly built virtually empty hut, destined to be an office block. So empty was this hut that we built a proscenium arch, rigged curtains and flood lights and under the critical direction of Doc John, rehearsed "A Respite", a very dubious midwinter show for which I wrote several even more dubious songs. Because the hut was undeveloped in terms of the offices for which it had been built, we were undisturbed in the preparations and for many of our invited guests, the result was a major surprise. Comments from the floor assured us that our efforts were more than well received, but as soon as the show finished, the proscenium came down and it was back to work on the sledges.

The following year, after the completion and inhabitation of the office block, we lacked such spacious luxury, and overhauling the sledges seemed a daunting prospect. But overhauling was still necessary as the doom of the huskies was still four years in the future and not contemplated by us. Wherever we might be permitted to a work, possibly one end of the dining room, the lounge at a pinch (but highly doubtful), most probably the chippy shop (carpenter's workshop), it would mean one sledge at a time being brought in, refurbished and then hauled back out. We would not be able to get a good production line set up, and more importantly, it would be difficult to have more than two people working at any one time.

And then we remembered the Old Base. Technically it had now been abandoned and the access shaft would be drifted up, but being relatively close to the surface it might be possible to dig out.

In late May '68 Peter Clarkson, Norris Riley and I paid a brief visit and found that the base was just accessible but needed much snow clearance. The disheartening part was the state of the place inside. Though the hut was structurally sound, the last occupants had simply abandoned the place after their last job and last meal - and why not? If it was being abandoned and would sink never to be seen again, why bother washing up or throwing out the garbage? One lost rubbish dump was just as good (or bad) as two. Somewhat disheartened at the prospect of cleaning up we returned to Grillage Village, but a day later with a little extra labour from intrigued, gullible colleagues, we set about making the place rehabitable.

Norris volunteered to look after the major domestic needs of coaxing the old Enfield generator back to life to provide light and power, though it would not run to much heat. He also took on the role of cook for everything except breakfast (Norris found mornings a difficult concept). Nevertheless we were grateful as it released the rest of us for other work. After four days we felt we had a useable and liveable hut, after another three, we had removed or resited several internal walls and had a very useful workshop.

There was one particular difficulty in using the old base as a sledge work shop: its access shaft. Even when cleared of snow, the shaft and tunnel to which it led were still designed for six foot men, not four metre sledges. It proved impossible to manoeuvre them from the vertical shaft to the horizontal tunnel. One might imagine that simply digging away more snow would provide the required extra space but the framework of the shaft was steel bars and not easily removed - at least not if we wanted to retain the structure's strength in the upper reaches. The easier solution was to remove the sledge handlebars which allowed just sufficient room. They would have to be refitted later in the open air.

The first few sledges were successfully installed and the old base was formally renamed "Nansen House". With various colleagues I was to inhabit the resurrected hut for the next three months.

Refurbishing a dog sledge is not a particularly onerous or time consuming task. One dedicated man could strip, scrape and rebuild a sledge in two or three days, but dedication was the problem. Resurrecting a defunct base, maintaining its services and also continuing one's gash and dog feeding duties at the Village considerably hampered the work flow. There was, however, another significant intrusion in our sledge work schedule.

Soon after we had moved in, even before work on the Nansens had started, certain furry, four legged young ladies on base decided it was time to produce the work teams of two seasons hence. Lassie and Chalky had already whelped and their little broods were being kept warm on top of the Aga cooker at the Village. The previous year, a bitch had whelped successfully but had been returned to the outdoor spans before she had adequately recovered her strength and fat. She died of suspected hypothermia. To avoid this we knew the bitches had to be sheltered for much longer. We also knew that the cooks would not tolerate several cartons of pups on their kitchen range beyond the immediate novelty value.

Fidlet Harry Wiggans had scarcely yet worked with huskies but he knew about, and more importantly cared about, dogs. He immediately saw the potential of Nansen House and soon joined our team proving himself a very resourceful and valuable fid long before deep winter beset us. Using timbers gleaned from derelict parts of the old base he set about converting the defunct subglacial garage into a canine maternity ward by constructing crèche pens for the bitches and their expected pups. These pens were raised off the floor and a powerful fan heater was installed to blow warm air under them. Word of this husky heaven must have reached the spans for Lassie and Chalky were soon joined by Michelle, Françoise, Snowy and Teifi. Trixie and Flossie followed a little later. Several of the male dogs had obviously been enjoying life!

I had envisaged a quiet dedicated sledge workshop but it was not to be. After a few weeks of moderate sledge building and intense pup rearing I posted the following advert at the Village:

WINTER HOLIDAYS ?
Book now at
"NEON'S GROTTO"

* Own full time cook to delight your palette.
* Nansen House recreation room provides health giving activities based on the rhythm and the dynamic tension principles.
* Own electricity supply as safeguard against National Grid failure.
  [though our own supply was very unreliable]
* Morning tea at no extra charge
* Constant hot water.
  [we couldn't turn it off!]

ALSO At a discreet distance from the main centre

"LA SALLE DES CHIENNES"

with charming hostesses Michelle, Françoise, Snowy and Teifi who are eager to accommodate you.
Enjoy the delights of feminine company in the seclusion of their Roman heated boudoirs which also feature full room service.

I didn't get any takers - I suspect people guessed what the health giving activities involved, either that or they had heard about Norris's cooking.

One day, after a gash duty at the Village, I returned to enjoy a little solitude for writing and sleeping. Some of the older puppies had been moved to the ice tunnel outside Nansen House in an attempt to acclimatise them to the cold. When I went to feed them I was dismayed to see their sorry plight. They were huddled in a small wet lump of shivering misery. I picked the lot up and carried them into the work shop. There then followed a long battle between the pups and me... and I lost. At first I thought all was well as they started to dry out, but then they started to wee. Mop and bucket were sought but I could not keep up. It became pure slapstick, each pup purposefully waiting until I was looking elsewhere then he would trot to a corner, under a sledge, behind a bench, anywhere and produce another puddle. Eventually Harry arrived and sliding gracefully around the new skating rink we set about housing the pups properly. It meant losing half our work space but one only had to look at the steaming little bundles to realise that inanimate wooden sledges seemed rather less important.

One modification was to direct a fan powered vent pipe from above the kitchen stove down to floor level. As there was nearly always a burner on for something this ensured near constant moderately warm air for the pups. One little animal later decided to investigate the source of the heat and our evening meal was interrupted by plaintive whimpers from the vent pipe. The pup was in danger of losing his inquisitive little nose in the fan but we couldn't reach him and he didn't know how to back out. We had to dismantle the whole affair and shake him out.

A very puzzled puppy but relieved (in both senses) tottered back to his bed. Harry attended the problem by covering the open end of the vent with wire mesh but a couple of days later two more pups needed shaking out when they scratched off the cover and went exploring. We had good sledge dogs in the making for sure.

It was difficult to keep a full team of men working on the sledges and I was not a good example. I had a report to write. The account of the Shackletons reconnaissance, with route details, observations and depot information were still in note form in my field journal. They needed converting into a formal report for London and several other destinations.

Writing up an expedition report in the twenty first century is a relatively painless affair. Open the laptop, type out a draught, cut and paste, adjust, reword as necessary, run it through the spell check, add a self-calculating spread sheet with a few automatically produced charts to impress the reader and when happy, print off as many copies as required, all identical and perfectly legible.

It wasn't quite so easy in the 1960s. There were no such things as computers or even electronic typewriters. Step one required a hand written draft that would then be subjected to crossings out, pencilled additions, arrows showing where a sentence should be moved. Step two was to decide how many copies were needed. Work couldn't be "saved" and reprinted at the press of a button; every word, every letter had to be thumped out on a manual typewriter. The more copies needed the harder one had to thump the keys for every copy required its own twin sheets of typing and carbon paper stacked in the typewriter. We claimed that eight copies was the maximum possible but the seventh and eighth were scarcely legible.

Reconnaissance reports were also full of route bearings and distances. These "polar coordinates" as they are known even in non-polar regions, were then recalculated to produce rectangular coordinates, that is distances south and distances east that would facilitate plotting on a map. Every location required its own pair of coordinates to be calculated. A simple computer driven spreadsheet would have made the whole process quick, easy and error free. With no spreadsheet, there was no command to "sum up this column" or "apply this formula to every number in that column", every calculation, every plot was done individually and as every one was subject to human error, they had to be checked and double checked. The whole report writing process was extremely time consuming and in the winter of '68 took me away from the much needed field preparation work at Nansen House.

There was another issue affecting output; there was a certain despondency about the place that led to lethargy. Several of us felt devalued and discarded by London Office (no individual was ever named). We had done all we could on the Shackleton reconnaissance, we claimed we had proved the overland route but it was now abandoned. Moreover, there were no expeditions planned for us the following season.

Nevertheless the sledges were completed and the pups kept us engaged by providing increasing entertainment (or work). By the time we moved out there were nineteen of the the inquisitive, little creatures.

Puddle production had grown to lacustrine proportion.

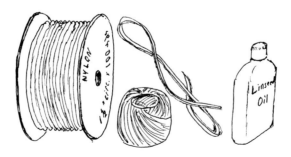

21 The Shacks

The writing of the Shackleton Reconnaissance report had seemed largely irrelevant and to confirm the abandonment of the Shacks, a small tractor party was instead despatched to lay depots for work in the Vestfjella, a range of mountains, some four hundred miles away and not yet fully surveyed. We all believed this new project was more a means of giving the geologists some rock to chip rather than any new or important work.

Even so I felt further alienation for although I was a field man and now had responsibility for the field store, I was not delegated to join the depot laying team. As some compensation Nick Mathys and I did take the Hairybreeks and lead the tractors through the Bob Pi. Logistically the allocation of personnel made sense as there were new men to train in tractor work, and I had my work cut out at Nansen House, but the hurt not the sense was felt at the time.

There then came what seemed like a final ending of all major expeditions organised by Halley Bay, for the Vestfjella expedition was itself called off and the recently established depots were abandoned.

Negotiations had been entered with the Americans and we learned that a four engined C130, possibly the same one we had seen over the Slessor Glacier, would fly to Halley the following season, collect six men with three dog teams and full equipment and fly them all to the Shackleton Range (the western end of the range not "our" mountains). It seemed we had indeed totally wasted our time with the dogs and tractors the previous season.

To add insult to injury, the team of six would consist of two geologists (Mike would be one of course), two surveyors who would fly in with the Americans, and two GAs (only one from our recce team). On hearing all this Nick and I had looked at each other: "Him or me?" we both thought. Golly resigned himself to disappointment being officially a carpenter not a GA. Nor would the 'kegs or big tractors be needed. It seemed the end of an era.

We Shacks recce men were left in limbo and it began to affect the morale of not just the dog and tractor men but the whole base.

On reading my reconnaissance report and assessing my conclusions, our base commander Chris, urged me to compile a brief supplementary report that could be transmitted to London by teleprinter. It read as follows:

The Case for the Shackletons

A reassessment of the situation regarding a
Shackleton tractor trip for Spring (Oct - Dec) 1968.

1   Furthest point reached by dog recce 80° 15' S, 16°16' W. [my calculation at the time]

2   Nunataks approx. 50 mls further west. Snow summits less than 50 mls SW. [actually far less]

3   These nunataks 480 mls from Halley.

4   Logistically possible to establish a depot and two working parties in the Eastern Nunataks, or larger depots for the next season (69/70).

5   Return depots for dog parties can also be laid.

6   There is already over £600 of good field equipment near the Slessor which could be lost after a two year lapse.
    [NB £600 is of course at 1968 prices - equivalent to about £9,000 in 2008]

7   There is less chance of picking up the beacon at 13/90 and the following route flags after a second winter.

8   Overall distance to Shacks not much greater than to Vestfjella.

9   Only 50 mls of route left to Shacks cf. 150 mls to be reccied in crevassed area to the Vestfjella.

10 Five of the team necessary for a trip this year ('68) were at the Slessor last year viz: field leader (Mathys), two who were on the final recce (Noble & Skidmore), driver (Gallsworthy), tractor mechanic who has worked with these vehicles for four seasons (Etchells).

11 Only one person on Base has been towards the Vestfjella, ie. to Tottans.

12 There will probably be no-one next year with field vehicle experience, and no-one at all with Etchell's field & large tractor experience.

13 No-one on Base next year ('69/70) will have travelled in the vicinity of the Slessor.

14 If contact is made with the geology party to be flown out, Clarkson (geologist) could stay the full season with GAs and dogs.

15 Regarding all aspects: knowledge of route, visibility of markers, preparedness of vehicles, experience, availability of men (who might otherwise be redundant), depots already laid, the most probable chance of reaching the Shackleton Range is this year (Spring '68).

16 All concerned are very keen on the Shacks and each department is confident of success.

Noble

I like to think this report to London, arguing the case for another attempt at the Shacks was persuasive. I suspect however that Sir Vivian, getting fed up with my protests and, more importantly realising that he had a team of experienced tractor men who would be kicking their heels all year said, "Might as well let the lads have go. They'll only cause a nuisance on base!"

A six man team was considered optimum for the planned four tractor expedition and Chris Sykes announced the members: Dad Etchells was an obvious choice, Stuart MacQuarrie (the tractor mechanic who replaced Chris when the latter was elevated to commander), John Carter (diesel mechanic), Norris Riley (new GA with too little dog or expedition experience to be dumped by air into the Shackletons in charge of a dog team and an even less experienced surveyor). Golly Gallsworthy was also asked to join the team and his delight was plain for all to see. The sixth man was to be an experienced GA… Nick Mathys… or me?

Nick, knowing how much the completion of the recce meant to me but also recognising the attraction of the air born trip to us both, graciously gave me the choice of air or overland. True the flight was very tempting, and true whoever went would enjoy real mountains with rocky ridges and cliffs! But… I chose the overland route with all its uncertainties. Sadly for Nick, he broke his leg shortly after landing in the Shacks and spent almost the entire time camp-bound with his leg in a plaster cast.

The team was set and I was called into the commander's office where I was invited to lead the expedition, an honour one doesn't accept lightly… but nor does one refuse.

The overland Shackletons expedition was now most definitely on, and preparations for the full 1968 field season began in earnest. Gone was the lethargy, gone the disillusionment, morale soared and I have rarely worked such long and continuous hours.

Not only were the Nansen sledges to be finished, with all that that entailed at Nansen House, I had to calculate and prepare the rations and camp equipment for several expeditions.

The "Air-Shacks" trip proved the most intricate as we were given a cargo weight limit for the C130 that I must not exceed. Throwing in ad hoc extra boxes of supplies, libraries of books or other uncalculated goodies could not be allowed. Every box of dog food was opened, the inner metal container discarded and the meat bars repacked in the lighter outer cardboard case. Every manfood box was opened, known surplus items such as the cocoa and at least one tin of butter were replaced by jam and sugar, and the soup supply was modified to give ten different varieties. Spares and emergency kits were reassessed and the inevitable extras that had been slowly and unnecessarily added over the years were all discarded.

The expedition was slimmed down to the bare minimum and I held the weight just within the given limit. It was therefore somewhat galling to me and no doubt very annoying for the team members when the air crew were surprised at how little kit was to be transported. "Plenty of room," the captain had said, "Want to take anything else? Don't you need a tractor or two?" Who dreamed up the weight limit I cannot imagine but it was obviously for a considerably smaller aircraft. Of course the C130 was built for major troop transportation so three lightweight Nansen's, twenty seven huskies and six sparsely equipped men with minimal rations scarcely compared with a whole platoon of soldiers in combat gear, complete with heavy armaments and jeeps. The C130 was not named the Hercules without reason. I'm sure however that the flight for our team was much more comfortable, and certainly more spacious than for the average squaddy. Being on expedition myself at the time I never knew if additional goodies were added but I received no complaints about the rations. Perhaps changing the soups had been sufficient!

Paul Coslett and Andy Wager with their separate, more local, glacial research parties were also due to take to the field, and although they could almost certainly be relied on to return every Saturday night for gin, beer and a film, they could not go out ill equipped. Tents, stoves, sleeping gear, sledges for their Skidoos and rations all had to be checked, repaired or replaced as necessary, and labelled as reserved for each trip.

There were other trips to cater for too. Many otherwise base-bound men needed holidays and in the better weather they would often take a spare dog team for a few days camping.

When it came to my own trip, my involvement in the preparation was somewhat less as I relied not just heavily but totally on Dad Etchells to ready the tractors, calculate our fuel needs, and assemble the spares and tools. I was nominally put in charge of the expedition but I knew that any decision or strategy I made would be subservient to the requirements of Dad and his tractors.

Even the camping was taken out of my hands as we planned a new approach. Some years earlier a workman's cabin had been supplied for establishing the temporary and very lonely "Coats Station". It had been mounted on a sledge and successfully towed some two hundred miles south onto the inland ice. It was later used during the darkening months of March and April '68 when it had been dragged to Mobster Creek for use as another temporary field base.

Doc Murray Roberts, who replaced John Brotherhood, had his own special interest - penguins, and Mobster Creek gave easy access to the sea ice where an enormous rookery collected every year. The cabin or "caboose" as it was initially known was fitted out with a couple of bunks, chairs and cooking area but was very spartan and during the brief time I accompanied Doc Murray, I found it pretty cold and inhospitable. In retrospect, our experience must have paled into insignificance compared with that of Phil Goodwin (meteorologist) and Lawrence Dicken (ionospherics) who were marooned (intentionally) at Coats Station from November '64 to (unintentionally) March '65.

The caboose's potential was obvious and Golly set to work converting this ex-ionospherics observatory, ex-penguin research base into a rather luxurious caravan that earned the title "Golly's Folly". This was to be the accommodation for the full Shackletons overland team that had been set at six men. There was a door at the front and small windows on each side wall. Across the blank end Golly erected a three tier set of bunks that would accommodate John Carter, Norris Riley and John Gallsworthy himself. Above and below the right hand window a double bunk for Stuart MacQuarrie and myself. Opposite in respectful solitude was Dad Etchells. The bunks of both Dad and myself served as seating for the collapsible table that could be erected between. In a corner by the door was the kitchen: an aluminium work top with a couple of primus stoves secured in place. That left one corner with a cupboard for stores in use and other daily essentials.

An attempt had been made to insulate the walls and roof, and even double glaze the windows, but any really effective insulation would have seriously reduced the accommodation space. To counteract the heat loss Golly commissioned electrician Geoff Smith who introduced heat in no uncertain form. A powerful paraffin burning, electrically ignited and driven fan heater was mounted on the outside back wall with a duct leading through the wall to vent under the lowest bunk. It could get very hot in Golly's Folly.

There were two other nice touches added by Geoff: in addition to a light over the kitchen and the table area, each bunk was given its own reading light, all powered by a cable from a pair of tractor batteries. No doubt those lights were used someday, but it was long after the return of the Shacks party. Perhaps Geoff had forgotten, when installing the lights in the twenty four hour winter dark, that the expedition would take place in twenty four hour summer sun!

A good radio receiver and a Squadcall were bolted to the wall beside the food cupboard and a near constant water supply was effected by securing a pressure cooker in a frame over a primus stove. The arrangement allowed snow to be melted under way.

There was another useful item though perhaps a nicety: an anemometer (wind speed indicator) was mounted just beside my bed head. When my alarm woke me, I could open my eyes, glance at the gauge and if it read more than fifteen knots, the speed at which generally the spindrift is too high for us to see the ground, I would roll over for another forty winks! The others, if awake would watch my move and do likewise. For those not awake it didn't matter.

The final adaptation was at my insistence. The tow bar "A" frame of the caboose sledge was boarded over to allow safe access and egress while on the move. I did not want to risk a second episode of falling into the gap.

Golly's Folly was an enormous success such that on the return trip, which for some reason enjoyed a considerably smoother ride, we were able to sleep and cook whilst under way. This had not been at all possible on the outward journey due to the lift and thump, lift and thump over the many sastrugi.

Whilst Golly was constructing his Folly, Dad, JC and Stuart were overhauling and preparing not two but four tractors. This was to be a major expedition. Not only would we have two Muskegs but two Internationals would attempt the journey also. They had never been used for expeditionary work before and their effectiveness was as unknown as the Shackletons themselves. Their addition gave us a load capacity of twenty nine tons spread over twelve cargo sledges and we would need every kilogram.

The preparation of our tractors did not just mean servicing but adding various essentials. It was found for instance that under full load the Internationals would go heel down and potentially dig themselves into a hole. A very simple answer was devised: two full fuel drums were wired to the bulldozer blades and this counterbalance solved the problem; it also gave an emergency supply of fuel.

Operating with such vehicles a long way from base, we had also to take a veritable garage of tools and spares. When one considers that, on the high plateau, the mechanics fitted a new hydraulic pipe, new water pump, replaced a glow plug, renewed a cracked fuel line, fitted a prop shaft and fan belt, such kit was essential. In addition there were regular twelve hour services when all sump and gear box oil was drained and replenished. Taking tractors into the field successfully is no mean achievement and Dad and his team, the stalwarts of the Black Gang, are to be praised.

Not only did they keep all the vehicles running efficiently, they provided for all foreseeable emergencies. We carried crevasse bridging girders, heavy duty block and tackles, wire ropes, winches, blow lamps, a large metal work vice welded to one of the Internationals, engine spares of every kind and an embarrassment of spanners and hammers, wrenches and screwdrivers. This load was small change however compared to the one hundred drums of avtur and petrol: four thousand five hundred gallons in all. Tractors that pull heavy loads, that rarely get out of second gear and have inefficient traction on soft surfaces, are exceptionally thirsty. Averaging one mile per gallon per tractor those four thousand five hundred gallons promised only one thousand one hundred and twenty five miles. The Shacks were estimated at a one thousand miles round trip; there would not be much fuel to spare. Even so, of the twenty nine ton load, eighteen tons were fuel! We were setting out on the heaviest, longest tractor journey ever undertaken by the British Antarctic Survey. What we were not to know was that within a decade such massive expeditions would be outdated even by overland treks for in 1978 Peter Witty and Mike Pinnock set out on the exact same journey with just one skidoo pulling a half ton load and travelling at five times our snail pace - such was the development in power and reliability of the skidoo.

In 1968 however, as we were forging our route south at a steady two miles per hour, a rather speedier expedition was launched elsewhere - nine thousand times speedier. Frank Borman, James Lovell and William Anders blasted off on the first flight to orbit the Moon! I later saw a breakdown of the weights of their Apollo 8 mission and was amazed to see that the ratios of fuel to vehicles to payload were almost identical to our own - there was however a slight difference in distance travelled!

After our hard fought reconnaissance of the previous year, after the hard and prolonged persuasion of London office, after the detailed and urgent planning and fitting out of caboose and tractors, the actual overland traverse to the Shacks was almost an anticlimax. It was nevertheless a very acceptable anticlimax being largely uneventful - just what a well-executed expedition should be.

The Bob Pi crossing was no problem and then Norris navigated us accurately the 200 plus miles across the totally featureless ice cap to depot 13/90. Another 54 miles and we homed in on Golly's Castle which proudly guarded depot 13/117 and which, despite the winter gales, still celebrated Christmas with its cardboard tree that now leaned jauntily south west, optimistically pointing the way to the mountains.

There we collected the entire depot supplies that half a year earlier I had thought would be totally lost, and somewhat surprisingly we were then able to follow the line of several old snow cairns to "Cathedral Cairn" that was still very prominent. Here, 400 miles from Halley a major time and fuel saving ploy was proposed by Dad. Our loads were now so lightened by the several tons of fuel that had been burned to date or depoted for the return that only two tractors were needed. As the Muskegs were faster and rather lighter, the Internationals and their sledges were parked up, their remnant loads transferred to the kegs and we continued now on a direct line for the mountains.

Leaving the big tractors behind saved us about ten drums of their diesel (avtur) - some 400 gallons. The savings on Muskeg petrol for the return journey would however be even greater and more significant for our objective. We realised that when we got back to the International tractors the two Muskegs could be driven onto a couple of empty sledges and towed back to to the Bob Pi Crossing a petrol saving of 700 gallons! With so much spare fuel we could have reached the South Pole(!) but more importantly we had a massive reserve for operating in the mountains and for depoting for future trips.

With plenty of petrol for the kegs, ample food and particularly time to spare (we were two weeks ahead of the permitted schedule), nothing was going to stop us now and a significant moment for me was passing Point Touché with its special snow pillar "Llareggub"; the name cribbed from Dylan Thomas at a time of frustrated ambition. Frustration was at last to be overcome and after a total journey of 500 miles, "Depot Dad" was established at the foot of a major nunatak (rock summit) of the Shackleton Range.

The bosses said the Shackletons
were well beyond our range,

They did, convinced, they did.
But preparations went ahead
    in case their minds should change,
And they did, and winced, they did.
Four tractors and twelve sledges with
    a twenty nine ton load,
One hundred drums of fuel which we
    hoped would not explode,
Bright marker flags we staked en route
    to show the homeward road,
We did, 'twas sense, we did.

At fifteen hundred revs we clocked up
    two miles every hour,
We did, so slow, we did.
High speed we could not ask for
    when our tractors gave us power,
And they did, to tow, they did.
We trundled on across the high
    plateau both day and night,
Our objective, those mountains gave us
    not one single sight,
We thought we saw them last year, now we
    hoped that we were right,
We did, just so, we did.

Our fuel quickly dwindled as we
    depoted it on route,
It did, just dropped, it did.
So when the loads were light enough,
    two tractors went to boot,
They did, they stopped, they did.
Just one minor problem was the
    glacier in the gap

Between us and those mountains which are
    not on any map,
We thanked our stars that there was no
    crevassing on that lap,
We did, we hoped, we did.

Just three weeks after leaving base
    we spied a mountain top
We did, hopes raised, we did.
With mountains now in sight we drove
    without single stop,
We did, trail blazed, we did.
Five hundred miles we travelled on a
    route not run before,
Now we had reached the Shackletons
    our aim was to explore,
But soon we had to head for home,
    five hundred miles in store,
We did, eyes glazed, we did

The bosses said that what we'd done was
    most important work,
They did, we heard, they did.
But we agreed that it's the kind
    of job we would not shirk,
We did, my word, we did.
Eight weeks upon a holiday
    with peace and lots of sleep,
Though we were counting fuel drums
    instead of counting sheep,
The drivers woke at intervals
    their direction to keep,
They did, when stirred, they did!

There had been a couple of occasions when drivers had fallen asleep. Dad Etchells, in the lead vehicle, dozed off and was seen executing a long graceful turn in the direction of the Pole of Inaccessibility. There was some concern as no tractor could catch him and the snow at that point was too soft for anyone to outrun him on foot. Would he continue and describe a giant circle unaware? would he awake somewhere over the horizon and be unable to work out where he was or how to rejoin us? I was just about to say we all ought to follow and we would sort out a route correction later, when Dad's tractor commenced another graceful curve back on course. I decided it was desirable for there to be two people in the lead vehicle in future!

Stuart MacQuarrie was the other culprit. One of the problems with tracked vehicles on snow is that the two tracks do not drive with the same efficiency. One side may just slip a little more in slightly softer snow, or more noticeably, if the sun was shining on one side ice built up on the opposite shaded track sometimes causing slippage, sometimes increasing the diameter of the drive wheel. The net result, whatever the cause, was that all the tractors veered off course and needed constant correction (the cause of Dad's gentle detour); but unlike a car one could not set the steering wheel to compensate, every few minutes one had to apply the brake lever to the overrunning side. A moderately effective solution was found: one placed one's vehicle in the tracks of the sledge train in front. These acted like tram lines such that the trailing vehicle tended to follow the tracks.

This was the technique that Stuart adopted, but two miles an hour with no variation in scenery and a warm cab is very soporific. Stuart awoke to find his own tractor mounting the rear cargo sledge of the train ahead that had stopped to plant a route flag. "So that's where little Nansens and Skidoos come from," some wit observed.

I had a near miss with a similar incident when I got too engrossed in the James Bond I was reading!

Five weeks we had allowed for the journey out, three it had taken, so a fortnight remained to explore the area. "The Shackleton Range" sounds big and impressive but the reality is that the Eastern Shacks (later named Pioneers Escarpment) were quite small isolated nunataks reaching a maximum height of 1370 metres, and of this barely 300 metres protruded above the ice cap. Nevertheless six summits were ascended, summits on mountains never before seen from ground level, and only once or twice spotted from the air. Rock samples were collected for the geologists, currently at the other end of the range. A preliminary survey map was made and all the significant features named.

Perhaps I didn't expect many of our allocated names to be taken seriously, especially those that were geologically incorrect but it would have been nice to be consulted when the official map was subsequently produced. All our chosen names were disallowed by the self-important Place Names Committee! Mount Shelleen, a tongue in cheek honouring of Dad Etchells, the spitting image of Kid Shelleen in his long-johns, became Lundstrøm Knoll; the aggressively shaped Fang was filed down to Jackson Tooth; the isolated Lonely Mountain was ambivalently renamed Mount Dewar, and the eponymous Red Hill that was covered with garnets paled to Blanchard Hill! Where the imagination of committees? Where the romance of discovery? Where the long held tradition of explorers naming their finds? Where the basic courtesy? That one high handed dismissal of our efforts still niggles after forty years.

A niggle it might be, but as we ascended those wonderful pristine mountains, nothing was further from my mind. I simply revelled in my good fortune to be where I was, doing what many can only dream about. I felt both humble and honoured. The place, the scenery, the light and colour, the solitude, the clean unsullied virginity, the whole ambience was magnificent.

A hundred miles to the west were the outlines of the main range where the airborne team was working, to east and north and hidden by distance, scale and a year's snow fall, the old sinuous tracks of a few tiny tractors and even tinier dog teams. The whole southern panorama was something else: a whole new unexplored horizon with one very intriguing prominence in the far distance... Some day? but no, this was where it stopped for me and indeed for us all. A visit to that unknown, unnamed, distant mountain would have to await some future probably airborne team. Our task had been to find a route to the remote Eastern Shackleton mountains and that we had done. It was the culmination of not just our two years of our effort, but the cumulative effort of all the men who had built up our collective knowledge and experience over the previous years.

As I skied back across the snow field below our final summit, psyching myself up to leave the Shackletons, to leave this amazing dream-come-true and commence the long journey home, I thought fondly of my old friends: the dogs. It would have been good to share our success with Whisky and Shem and the others, for they had made it all possible. Without their hard work the previous year we would not have scaled these mountains nor delighted in these incredible vistas.

Little did I realise as we trundled "home" across the high plateau that our reconnaissance journeys to the Shackletons, first by dogs and Muskegs, and then this pure tractor traverse, would be the last major expeditions from Halley. Although Warden and Flick would, in 1971, establish a "furthest north" by dog sledge on the Riiser Larsen Ice Shelf, and considerable work, mainly by skidoo, would continue for several more years on the local ice shelf, the great days of exploratory travel were over. The 1960s had been a golden era at our remote Antarctic survey station. The snows accumulated year after year, first drifting over and obliterating our tracks then deepening and submerging the route cairns and flags and finally overwhelming the tall depot stakes, the fuel and supplies they marked now lost forever beneath the all consuming ice.

The Tottanfjella, Heimfrontfjella, Vestfjella, the Therons and the Shackletons had been surveyed, *geologised,* studied and recorded, but now they returned to their pristine solitude. It was as though we had never been.

At home in England I am always reminded of those wonderful, soul shaping days every time a *sun dog* eyes me from the high cirrus clouds, or I see the pinks and mauves of a crisp winter's evening sky; but especially do I recall jewelled days amid the polar snows when my wife wears her unique and very special jewellery: a pendant necklace with matching earrings fashioned of "Adventurine", a delicate green rock that I won from a lonely buttress in the Shackleton Mountains.

South, my direction steer
South, where the air is clear,
Let me roam where the glaciers glisten,
I'm missin' ice and snow,
South, I want to go

South, in the crystal blue,
South, where my dreams came true,
Though frost may bite and fingers freeze
It eases my heart to be,
South, where my spirit's free

South, 'neath the midnight sun
South, where the dog teams run,
I don't want no dusky maiden,
My husky team will do
South, 'fore my days are through.

Epilogue

It is the summer of 2008 and I have just discovered that there is a small group of summits in the Norwegian sector of the Eastern Shackletons that bear my name: "Nobleknausane". I am briefly tempted to amend my criticism of the Place Names Committee in chapter 21 but it holds true: back in the 60s and 70s they were quite arrogant, or perhaps just socially naive. So, is it an honour having a mountain with one's name on it? Hardly since there was obviously no honour intended. No, the reality I have to accept is that new names were needed for newly mapped features and our team provided a neat set. It was like our use of Scottish islands when naming Huskies!

So there it is, Nobleknausane, 80°40'S 19°47'W, a remote group of summits that I never visited, never saw, nor even dreamed about... or so I thought...

And now I awake this morning with a dream and a picture in my head. The dream is one I had had on a mountain top forty years previous: *The whole southern panorama was something else: a whole new unexplored horizon with one very intriguing prominence in the far distance... Some day?* (page 190) The photo is one I had taken looking southeast from Mt Shelleen (Lundstrøm Knoll). Yes there on the horizon is that distant mountain top. I call up Google Earth on my laptop, plot in the coordinates for Nobleknausane and draw a line from there to Mt Shelleen. There was no doubt... the *very intriguing prominence* is Nobleknausane. I may not have visited them but I have both seen them and dreamed about them.

Nobleknausane can just be discerned, centre horizon, in the penultimate photo "Snow hills of the Eastern Shackletons..."

Appendix 1

Personae Dramatis of the Dog Days (1961 - 72)

The list below includes only those men who feature in my story; many others are included in the travel appendix. My apologies to any who feel miffed at being omitted but with several hundred men stationed at Halley during the dog days where do you stop?

Change over of personnel was every January so "67/68" means a two year tour from January 1967 to January 1969.
The position of Base Leader was redesignated Base Commander in 1967.

GA of course was the ubiquitous General Assistant

Ardus	Dennis	Glaciologist	60/61
Bailey	Jeremy	Geophysicist	'65 died in crevasse
Baker	Tony	Carpenter	64/65 67/68
Baldwin	Colin	Halley 2 Architect	3 wks 67
Blackwell	Bruce	Diesel mechanic	71/72
Blakeley	Peter	Tractor mechanic	'66
Bowra	Gordon	Doctor	63/64
Brooke	Dave	Geologist	66/67
Brotherhood	John / Doc	Doctor / physiologist	'67
Burgin	Mike	Physiologist technician	'67
Bury	Ian	Cook	71/72
Campbell	Iain	Doctor	'72
Carter	John / JC	Diesel mechanic	67/68/69
Chalmers	Jim	Geophysicist	68/69
Chinn	Ricky	Base Commander	'68
Clarkson	Peter	Geologist / Base Commander	68/69
Coslett	Paul	Glaciologist	67/68
Cotton	Phil	Surveyor / Base Leader	64/65
Cuthbertson	Dick	Diesel mechanic	'66
Dicken	Lawrence	Ionosphericist	64/65
Donaldson	Jack	GA	'72
Easty	David	Doctor	'61
Etchells	Alan / Dad	Tractor mechanic	63/64 & 67/68
Fletcher	David	GA	'72
Fry	John	Physiologist	'68
Fuchs	Sir Vivian	Director of BAS	58/73
Gallsworthy	John / Golly	Carpenter	67/68
Goodwin	Philip	Meteorologist	64/65
Haynes	Patrick	Cook / GA	65/66
Hill	David	Builder / carpenter	'67

Jamieson	Jim	Geophysicist	67/68
Jarman	Mike	Base Leader	61/62
Johnson	Colin	Base Leader	60/61
Johnston	Alan	Surveyor	66/67
Jones	Eric	Radio Operator	'61
Juckes	Lewis	Geologist	64/65
Laidlaw	Bill	Meteorologist	67/68
Lee	Bob	GA Tractors	61/62
Lovegrove	Geoff	Surveyor	65/66
MacQuarrie	Stuart	Tractor mechanic	'68
Mallinson	Gordon	Radio Operator	63/64
Mann	Neville	Surveyor	'63 lost on sea ice
Mathys	Nick	GA	67/68
Noble	Peter / Neon	GA	67/68
Pinnock	Mike	Ionosphericist	77/78 & 81
Porter	Jo	GA	'67
Precious	Alan	Meteorologist	'61
Ramage	Gordon	Tractor mechanic	'72
Roberts	Murray / Doc	Doctor/physiologist	68/69
Riley	Norris	GA	68/69
Ross	Ian	Geologist	'65
Russell	Simon	Radio operator	64/65
Samuel	Milne / Sam	Surveyor	63/64 & 66/67
Shirtcliffe	Jim	Builder	'68
Skidmore	Mike	Geologist	67/68
Skilling	John	Carpenter	'61
Sloman	Bill	Personnel officer (London)	'56/'78
Smith	Alan / Big Al	Builder	'67
Smith	Geoff / Abdul	Electrician	67/68/69
Stoneham	Toby	Tractor mechanic	71/72
Swift	Brian	Radar mechanic	'66
Sykes	Chris	Tractor mechanic / BC	67/68
Thomas	Bob	Glaciologist	66/67
Thornton	Edwin	Meteorologist	61/62
Wager	Andy	Glaciologist	'68
Wharton	Paul	Electrician	'67
Whiteman	Paul	Meteorologist 62/63 Base Ldr	'66
Wiggans	Harry	GA	68/69
Wild	Dai	Surveyor	64/65 died in crevasse
Wilson	John	Doctor	'65 died in crevasse
Witty	Peter	Diesel mechanic /BC	'77 & 79
Wornham	Colin	Meteorologist / GA	66/67
Worsfold	Dick	Geologist	63/64
Wright	Graham	GA	69/70

Appendix 2

Field Expeditions from Halley Bay - 1957 to 1972

Writers of journey reports were given no formal layout to follow and there was no insistence upon detailed cross referencing with earlier reports, consequently authors (myself included) often omitted information that would be *taken as read* at the time but might not be evident to later generations. In geographical descriptions we often did not allow for the ever-changing nature of the ice shelf nor of the changing research projects and perhaps did not realise that many names and places would be quite transient; their locations and significance sometimes lost.

In addition many authors included several journeys, which involved several different men, in a single report. Trying to identify the individual journeys, the men who undertook those journeys and their destinations proved a difficult task. There were also, inevitably, a number of holiday jaunts, particularly with dogs, that may have been of longer duration and covering greater distances than some of the reported scientific trips but they were never recorded. To readers who search this appendix for specific names and specific journeys and fail to find them I can only apologise and invite them to supply the missing information.

Field Expeditions from Halley Bay - 1957 to 1972

Expeditions are credited to the year in which they commenced. Unless otherwise stated all journeys start and finish at Halley. The number of expeditions is a little misleading as a single expedition sometimes involved several individual journeys. I have counted discreet sections or phases as separate expeditions as with the 1965 Heimfronfjella expedition and the 1968 Shackletons reconnaissance.

Overall totals - Expedition reports held by BAS record that over this period **206** expeditions were run involving **307** teams or vehicles for a combined time of **4346** days and involving **205** men.

Year/exped.	Depart	Return	Days	Type	Units	Destination	Personnel
57 /1	21.4.1957	21.4.1957	1	Manhaul	1	Shelf	W Bellchambers, J Burton, L Constantine
57 /2	31.8.1957	2.9.1957	3	Manhaul	1	Shelf	W Bellchambers, J Burton, D Harrison
57 /3	15.9.1957	21.9.1957	7	Manhaul	1	Shelf	L Constantine, H Dyer
57 /4	1.11.1957	4.11.1957	4	Manhaul	1	Shelf	R Smart, W Bellchambers, J Burton
57 /5	28.11.1957	30.11.1957	3	Manhaul	1	Shelf	P Brennan, L Barclay
57 /6	2.12.1957	4.12.1957	3	Manhaul	1	Shelf	L Barclay, J Burton, D Harrison
Totals for year 1957			21	6	6		
58 /1	2.3.1958	16.3.1958	15	Manhaul	1	Shelf	L Constantine, P Brennan
58 /2	19.11.1958	28.11.1958	10	Manhaul	1	Shelf	L Barclay, P Brennan plus Stumpy (dog)
58 /3	1.12.1958	3.12.1958	3	Manhaul	1	Shelf	J Burton, E Gane, D Harrison
Totals for year 1958			28	3	3		

Year/exped.	Depart	Return	Days	Type	Units	Destination	Personnel
59 / 1	8.11.1959	13.11.1959	6	Manhaul	3	Shelf	J Norman, M Artz, A Hedderly, W Whitehall
Totals for year 1959			6	1	3		
60 / 1	9.11.1960	11.11.1960	3	Manhaul	2	Shelf	A Lewis, G Moore
60 / 2	19.11.1960	29.11.1960	11	Manhaul	2	Shelf	D Ardus, C Johnson plus Stumpy (dog)
60 / 3	4.12.1960	15.12.1960	12	Manhaul	2	Shelf	G Moore, M Taplin
Totals for year 1960			26	3	6		
61 / 1	12.3.1961	15.3.1961	4	Dogs	1	Shelf	E Jones, M Jarman
61 / 2	15.3.1961	19.3.1961	5	Dogs	1	Hinge zone	A Precious, D Ardus
61 / 3	21.3.1961	9.4.1961	20	Dogs	2	Hinge zone	A Precious, D Ardus, C Johnson, D Easty
61 / 4	13.4.1961	17.4.1961	5	Dogs	1	Shelf	C Dean, C Johnson
61 / 5	5.9.1961	20.9.1961	16	Dogs	1	Shelf	C Johnson & M Taplin
61 / 6	24.9.1961	27.9.1961	4	Muskeg	1	Shelf	D Jehan, R Lee, J Skilling, M Brittain, B Peters, A Thorne-Middleton, PJ Noble, S Marsden
61 / 7	30.9.1961	11.10.1961	12	Muskeg	1	Shelf	G Talmage, C Johnson
61 / 8	20.10.1961	31.10.1961	12	Manhaul	1	Shelf	D Easty & G Moore
61 / 9	20.10.1961	9.12.1961	51	Dogs	1	Tottanfjella (direct)	D Ardus & C Johnson (First route through the hinge zone & first men to reach any mountains (Tottanfjella) from Halley, also longest ever unaccompanied journey from Halley)
61 / 10	29.10.1961	3.11.1961	6	Muskeg	1	Shelf	D Jehan, C Dean, E Jones
61 / 11	5.11.1961	30.11.1961	26	Manhaul	1	Shelf	M Bethel, E Docchar, D Edwards, E Thornton (First manhaul crossing of the Hinge Zone)
61 / 12	2.12.1961	9.12.1961	8	Dogs	1	Shelf	M Sumner & M Thurston

Year/exped.	Depart	Return	Days	Type	Units	Destination	Personnel
61/13	5.12.1961	16.12.1961	12	Manhaul	1	Shelf	B Peters, G Moore, S Marsden
61/14	20.12.1961	27.12.1961	8	Dogs	1	Shelf	M Taplin & G Blundell
61/15	27.12.1961	6.1.1962	11	Dogs	2	Inland Ice	A Precious, D Easty, E Jones, J Skilling (First crossing of Hinge Zone on a viable tractor route - later called the Bob Pi Crossing)
Totals for year 1961			200	15	17		
62/1	11.1.1962	14.1.1962	4	Dogs	1	Shelf	C Dean, G Blundell, G Moore
62/2	24.1.1962	26.1.1962	3	Dogs	1	Shelf	M Brittain & M Jarman
62/3	20.2.1962	20.2.1962	1	Muskeg	1	Bob Pi Crossing	R Lee & M Jarman (Bob & Pi) (First tractor crossing of Hinge Zone following the route of Precious & party - known as the Bob Pi)
62/4	23.2.1962	1.3.1962	7	Dogs	1	Hinge Zone	G Blundell & M Winterton
62/5	16.3.1962	29.3.1962	14	Dogs	1	Hinge Zone	M Bethell & M Winterton
62/6	26.3.1962	31.3.1962	6	Dogs	1	Shelf	D Finlayson & E Thornton
62/7	26.3.1962	31.3.1962	6	Dogs	1	Shelf	B Peters & M Jarman
62/8	9.9.1962	10.10.1962	32	Dogs	1	Stancombe Wills Glacier	E Thornton & P Blakely
62/9	29.9.1962	1.10.1962	3	Dogs	1	Shelf	B Peters & M Jarman
62/10	14.10.1962	20.10.1962	7	Dogs	1	Hinge Zone	R Lee & M Jarman
62/11	17.10.1962	29.10.1962	13	Muskeg	2	Tottanfjella	C Brown, K Lambert, J Griffiths, C Spaans, J Hill, R Dean
62/12	24.10.1962	24.12.1962	62	Dogs	1	Hinge Zone	M Winterton & S Marsden, then Winterton & M Blundell (see 62/13)

Year/exped.	Depart	Return	Days	Type	Units	Destination	Personnel
62/13	5.11.1962	12.11.1962	8	Muskeg	2	Bob Pi	C Brown, P Whiteman, D Finlayson, F Bent, C Ruffell, M Blundell (out), S Marsden (back) (see 62/12)
62/14	5.11.1962	15.11.1962	11	Dogs	1	Bob Pi	B Peters & J Holt
62/15	14.11.1962	19.11.1962	6	Manhaul	1	Bob Pi to Halley	F Bent & C Ruffell (taken out by muskeg - see 62/13)
62/16	18.11.1962	25.11.1962	8	Dogs	1	Bob Pi	B Peters & J Holt
62/17	28.11.1962	3.12.1962	6	Manhaul	1	Shelf	S Marsden, C Ruffell, R Dean, C Spaans, P Whiteman
62/18	30.11.1962	15.12.1962	16	Dogs	1	Bob Pi recce	M Bethell & D Robinson
62/19	27.12.1962	29.12.1962	3	Dogs	1	Shelf	P Blakeley, M Jarman
Totals for year 1962			216	19	21		
63/1	7.1.1963	16.1.1963	10	Dogs	1	Bob Pi recce	E Thornton & C Brown
63/2	2.3.1963	27.3.1963	26	Dogs	1	Bob Pi recce	M Winterton & G Bowra
63/3	6.3.1963	27.3.1963	22	Muskeg Eliason	2 2	Inland Ice (vehicle testing)	A Etchells & J Holt, D Jehan & M Samuel M Sumner & N Mann, G Mallinson & R Worsfold
63/4	11.9.1963	17.10.1963	37	Muskeg	2	Tottanfjella reconnaissance	A Etchells & N Brind, D Jehan & H O'Gorman (dropped one keg in Bob Pi crevasse - unable to recover with remaining keg. Success with assistance of M Sumner & B Krachenbucki in another keg.
63/5	10.10.1963	7.4.1964	181	Dogs	2	Tottanfjella (see 63/8)	OUT: M Samuel & G Bowra, R Worsfold & M Winterton. BACK: R Worsfold & M Samuel, C Bowra & G Mallinson on 9th Nov Mallinson replaced Winterton

Year/exped.	Depart	Return	Days	Type	Units	Destination	Personnel
63 /6	18.10.1963	21.10.1963	4	Dogs	1	Shelf	J Holt & D Hollas
63 /7	27.10.1963	29.10.1963	3	Muskeg	1	Shelf	D Finlayson, D Petrie, M Walford
63 /8	3.11.1963	17.11.1963	15	Muskeg	2	Tottanfjella (see 63/5)	OUT: A Etchells & M Sumner, P Whiteman & G Mallinson BACK: A Etchells & M Sumner, P Whiteman & M Winterton on 9th Nov Winterton replaced Mallinson
63 /9	29.11.1963	12.12.1963	14	Dogs	1	Shelf	D Finlayson, D Petrie, M Walford
63 /10	15.12.1963	20.12.1963	6	Manhaul	1	Shelf	D Hollas & J Westwood
Totals for year 1963			318		10	16	
64 /1	20.3.1964	8.4.1964	20	Muskeg	3	Tottanfjella (depot laying)	Etchells & H Rogers, I Buckler, G Thomson
64 /2	10.9.1964	7.12.1964	89	Dogs	1	Heimfrontfjella (travelled out with 64/3)	M Samuel & P Cotton,
64 /3	10.9.1964	4.4.1965	207	Dogs	2	Heimfrontfjella (travelled out with 64/2)	OUT: R Worsfold & L Juckes, D Wild & A Baker BACK: S Russell & D Wild, L Juckes & A Baker Russell replaced Worsfold in field - see next entry.
64 /4	12.9.1964	3.11.1964	53	Muskeg	3	Heimfrontfjella (support for 64/2 & 3)	OUT: A Etchells, J Westwood, G Thompson, S Russell BACK: Etchells, Westwood, Thompson, R Worsfold
64 /5	9.11.1964	11.11.1964	3	Dogs	1	Shelf coast	D Petrie (solo)
64 /6	21.11.1964	7.12.1964	17	Muskeg	2	Ice Cap	B Krachenbuehl, W Bellchambers, G Thompson, G Bowra, L Dicken, P Goodwin (Caboose established as Coats Station manned by Dicken & Goodwin who were out 139 days)
64 /7	29.11.1964	5.12.1964	7	Eliason	1	Shelf coast	A Champness & M Turner

Year/exped.	Depart	Return	Days	Type	Units	Destination	Personnel
64 /8	11.12.1964	19.12.1964	9	Dogs	1	Hinge Zone	D Hollas & D George
Totals for year 1964			405	8	14		
65 /1	19.1.1965	21.1.1965	3	Eliason	1	Shelf coast	W Sievwright, BP Smith
65 /2	11.3.1965	8.4.1965	29	Muskeg	3	Ice Cap	J Wright & H Rogers, B Porter & J Bailey, D Beebe & P Cotton (Recovery of Dicken & Goodwin plus the caboose from Coats Station)
65 /3	30.5.1965	7.6.1965	9	Muskeg	2	Shelf	B Porter & B Barnes, D Beebe & A Weeks
65 /4	10.9.1965	8.12.1965	90	Muskeg Dogs	3 1	Heimfrontfjella (travelled out with 65/5 & 6)	OUT: D Beebe, I Ross, J Bailey, B Porter, L Juckes & J Wilson BACK: Porter, Ross, Juckes - dog team towed by the one remaining muskeg (Bailey and Wilson died when their muskeg fell into a crevasse, other 'keg broke down & left in field)
65 /5	10.9.1965	21.12.1965	103	Dogs	1	Heimfrontfjella (travelled out with 65/4 & 6)	OUT: D Wild & R Rhys-Jones, (Wild died with Wilson & Bailey - see above) BACK: D Beebe & R Rhys-Jones
65 /6	10.9.1965	15.4.1966	218	Dogs	1	Heimfrontfjella (travelled out with 64/4 & 5)	G Lovegrove & P Haynes (achieved longest endurance & longest journey from Halley - 218 days in the field & travelled 1560 miles)
65 /7	21.12.1965	24.12.1965	4	Muskeg Dogs	1 1	Hinge Zone	B Armstrong & M Sievwright, L Juckes & R Stokes
Totals for year 1965			456	7	14		

Year/exped.	Depart	Return	Days	Type	Units	Destination	Personnel
66/1	16.2.1966	2.3.1966	15	Dogs	1	Hinge Zone	C Wornham, R Thomas, R Lloyd
66/2	11.3.1966	8.5.1966	59	Dogs	1	Shelf	R Thomas & C Blossom
66/3	18.3.1966	2.4.1966	16	Dogs	1	Shelf	A Johnston & R Lloyd
66/4	27.3.1966	7.5.1966	42	Muskeg	2	Tottanfjella	M Samuel, D Brook, D Beebe, C Gostic (attempt to recover broken vehicle see 64/5)
66/5	18.8.1966	30.8.1966	13	Dogs	1	Inland Ice	C Read & R Thomas
66/6	17.9.1966	20.10.1966	34	Manhaul	1	Inland Ice	R Thomas & W Izatt
66/7	17.9.1966	22.10.1966	36	Muskeg	3	Tottanfjella	R Cuthbertson, P Haynes, B Swift, S Noble (recovered broken 'Keg see 65/4 & 66/4)
66/8	4.10.1966	13.12.1966	71	Dogs	3	Therons recce (followed by muskegs 66/9)	G Lovegrove & M Shaw, C Wornham & A Johnston, D Brook & D McKerrow
66/9	8.11.1966	25.12.1966	48	Muskeg	3	Therons (accompanied 66/8)	A Williams, P Blakely, P Haynes, M Samuel joined on return by G Lovegrove & M Shaw plus 1 dog team
66/10	15.11.1966	17.12.1966	33	Eliason	1	Hinge Zone	B Armstrong & R Thomas
66/11	13.12.1966	25.3.1967	103	Dogs	2	Work in Therons	C Wornham & A Johnston, D Brook & D McKerrow (see 66/8 & 9)
Totals for year 1966			470	11	19		
67/1	5.1.1967	23.1.1967	19	Eliason	1	Shelf	A Wilson & R Thomas
67/2	12.3.1967	8.4.1967	28	Eliason	1	Shelf	P Coslett, R Thomas, M Skidmore
67/3	15.8.1967	16.8.1967	2	Muskeg	1	Shelf	R Thomas, P Coslett
67/4	19.8.1967	23.8.1967	5	Dogs	1	Shelf	R Thomas, P Coslett

Year/ exped.	Depart	Return	Days	Type	Units	Destination	Personnel
67/5	28.8.1967	30.8.1967	3	Muskeg	1	Shelf	R Thomas, P Coslett
67/6	11.9.1967	14.12.1967	95	Dogs	1	Shelf	A Johnston, J Porter
67/7	26.9.1967	31.10.1967	36	Dogs	2	Bob Pi recce to Inland Ice (Shackletons recce phase 1 of 5)	C Wornham & PH Noble / M Skidmore, D Brook & N Mathys Skidmore replaced Noble in field by Skidoo driven by J Porter (seconded from 67/9)
67/8	26.9.1967	3.11.1967	39	Eliason Skidoo	1 1	Shelf	A Smith R Thomas
67/9	30.9.1967	26.10.1967	27	Skidoo	1	Shelf	P Coslett, C Gostick then J Porter
67/10	2.10.1967	14.10.1967	13	Dogs	1	Shelf	A Johnston, A Baker
67/11	24.10.1967	8.11.1967	16	Dogs	1	Shelf	A Johnston, K Halliday
67/12	28.10.1967	13.11.1967	17	Muskeg	2	Therons (Shackletons recce phase 2 of 5)	OUT: A Etchells & PH Noble, C Sykes & M Samuel COLLECTED en route: C Wornham & M Skidmore, D Brook & N Mathys, + 18 dogs! (see 67/8) BACK: A Etchells & PH Noble, C Sykes, M Skidmore
67/13	31.10.1967	9.11.1967	10	Skidoo	1	Shelf	P Coslett, C Blossom
67/14	31.10.1967	24.12.1967	55	Skidoo	1	Shelf	P Coslett, J Porter
67/15	5.11.1967	28.11.1967	24	Dogs	1	Work in Therons	C Wornham & D Brook (started in Therons - see 67/12)
67/16	9.11.1967	29.11.1967	21	Dogs	1	Therons to Slessor Glacier (Shackletons recce phase 3 of 5)	M Samuel & N Mathys (started from Therons - see 67/12)

Year/exped.	Depart	Return	Days	Type	Units	Destination	Personnel
67/17	13.11.1967	22.11.1967	10	Dogs	1	Shelf	A Wilson & M Baring-Gould
67/18	13.11.1967	25.11.1967	13	Skidoo	1	Inland ice	A Smith & C Gostick
67/19	13.11.1967	1.12.1967	19	Eliason	1	Shelf	P Coslett with J Porter / C Read / P Wharton / M Burgin / W Laidlaw Coslett's assistants were ferried out in turn
67/20	13.11.1967	4.12.1967	22	Eliason	3	Inland Ice	R Thomas, R Docchar / P Wharton / M Burgin
67/21	15.11.1967	21.11.1967	7	Dogs	1	Shelf	A Johnston, N Fothergill
67/22	23.11.1967	1.1.1968	40	Muskeg	2	Slessor Glacier (Shackletons recce phase 4 of 5)	OUT: A Etchells & PH Noble, J Gallsworthy, M Skidmore BACK: A Etchells, C Wornham, M Samuel, D Brook Change over of personnel at Slessor Glacier
67/23	24.11.1967	3.12.1967	10	Dogs	1	Shelf	A Williams & D McKerrow
67/24	2.12.1967	9.12.1967	8	Dogs	1	Shelf	A Johnston, J Jamieson
67/25	6.12.1967	10.12.1967	5	Dogs	1	Shelf coast	C Blossom & R Docchar
67/26	10.12.1967	23.12.1967	14	Eliason	1	Shelf coast	R Thomas & A Baker
67/27	11.12.1967	21.12.1967	11	Dogs	1	Shelf	J Carter & D Hill
67/28	13.12.1967	21.12.1967	9	Dogs	1	Shelf	G McWilliam & N Fothergill
67/29	31.12.1967	6.3.1968	67	Dogs	2	Slessor Head to furthest south & retn to Halley (Shacks recce phase 5 of 5)	N Mathys & J Gallsworthy, PH Noble & M Skidmore (starting at head of Slessor Glacier, Noble & Skidmore achieved app 80°30'S, leaving a 600 ml return journey by dog sledge)
Totals for year 1967			645	29	36		

Year/exped.	Depart	Return	Days	Type	Units	Destination	Personnel
68/1	20.2.1968	9.3.1968	19	Skidoo	1	Shelf	P Coslett & A Wager
68/2	13.3.1968	23.3.1968	11	Dogs	1	Bob Pi (leading 68/3)	PH Noble & N Mathys
68/3	13.3.1968	10.4.1968	29	Muskeg	2	Tottanfjella (depot laying)	A Etchells & P Clarkson, S MacQuarrie & H Wiggans
68/4	14.3.1968	29.3.1968	16	Skidoo	1	Shelf	P Coslett & A Wager
68/5	3.4.1968	15.4.1968	13	Skidoo	1	Shelf	P Coslett & N Riley
68/6	7.4.1968	13.4.1968	7	Dogs	1	Shelf	PH Noble & A Wager
68/7	21.4.1968	27.4.1968	7	Skidoo	1	Shelf	P Coslett & N Riley
68/8	29.4.1968	5.5.1968	7	Skidoo	1	Shelf	P Coslett & N Riley
68/9	23.9.1968	11.10.1968	19	Dogs	3	Bob Pi recce	PH Noble & N Riley, M Skidmore & P Clarkson, H Wiggans & W Laidlaw
68/10	9.10.1968	25.10.1968	17	Skidoo	1	Shelf	P Coslett, P Mountford, P Pitts
68/11	31.10.1968	26.11.1968	27	Skidoo	1	Inland Ice	P Coslett, K Gainey plus Eliason
68/12	31.10.1968	24.12.1968	55	Muskeg International	2 2	E Shackletons (Pioneer Escarpment)	PH Noble, A Etchells, J Carter J Gallsworthy, N Riley, S MacQuarrie (Largest and heaviest expedition ever mounted with 2 International tractors, 2 Muskegs, 12 sledges and 29 ton load)
68/13	5.11.1968	22.11.1968	18	Skidoo	1	Shelf	A Wager, C Platt
68/14	22.11.1968	26.1.1969	66	Aircraft Dogs	2 3	W Shackletons	N Mathys & A True, M Skidmore & P Clarkson, H Wiggans & K Blakelock (1st expedition air lifted to Shackletons by Americans. Lockheed C130 aircraft Blakelock flown to Halley for season then back out)
68/15	2.12.1968	13.12.1968	12	Skidoo	1	Shelf	P Coslett, D French, J Chalmers

Year/ exped.	Depart	Return	Days	Type	Units	Destination	Personnel
68 / 16	3.12.1968	27.12.1968	25	Skidoo	1	Shelf	A Wager, K Halliday
68 / 17	17.12.1968	27.12.1968	11	Skidoo	1	Shelf	P Coslett, J Fry
Totals for year 1968			359	17	27		
69 / 1	7.1.1969	15.1.1969	9	Skidoo	1	Shelf	P Coslett, J Gallsworthy
69 / 2	10.1.1969	17.1.1969	8	Skidoo	1	Shelf	A Wager, D Maclennan
69 / 3	17.2.1969	17.3.1969	29	Dogs	1	Shelf	N Riley, A Clayton, A True, M Macrae, H Wiggans
69 / 4	26.2.1969	2.3.1969	5	Dogs	1	Hinge Zone	H Wiggans & D Wilkins
69 / 5	10.3.1969	24.3.1969	15	Dogs	2	Shelf	H Wiggans & G Wright, D Wilkins & M Guyatt
69 / 6	24.3.1969	2.4.1969	10	Dogs	2	Shelf	H Wiggans, N Riley, C Clayton, A True, M Macrae
69 / 7	1.10.1969	11.10.1969	11	Dogs	2	Hinge Zone Ardus Johnson route	G Wright & N Riley, M Guyatt & A Clayton
69 / 8	15.10.1969	29.10.1969	15	Dogs	2	Bob Pi recce	H Wiggans & R Tiffin, G Wright & A True
69 / 9	17.10.1969	23.10.1969	7	Muskeg	2	Bob Pi	N Riley, R Palmer, M Macrae, I Smith
69 / 10	20.10.1969	25.10.1969	6	Dogs	1	Shelf	A Clayton & M Guyatt
69 / 11	1.11.1969	4.11.1969	4	Muskeg International	4 2	Bob Pi	N Riley, R Palmer, M Macrae I Smith, D Groom, D Hoy (International tractor lost in Bob Pi crevasse - depot laying aborted)
69 / 12	2.11.1969	8.11.1969	7	Dogs	1	Shelf	A Clayton & M Guyatt
69 / 13	4.11.1969	10.11.1969	7	Dogs	1	Shelf	H Wiggans & C Jones
69 / 14	4.11.1969	17.11.1969	14	Dogs	1	Shelf	D Wilkins & G Soar
69 / 15	12.11.1969	19.11.1969	8	Muskeg	2	Shacks route	R Palmer, I Smith, M Macrae, K Chappell

Year/exped.	Depart	Return	Days	Type	Units	Destination	Personnel
69/16	19.11.1969	25.1.1970	68	Aircraft Dogs	2 3	W Shacklletons	P Clarkson & H Wiggans, A True & G Wright, A Claytion & M Guyatt (2nd expedition air lifted to Shackleons by Americans. Lockheed C130 aircraft)
69/17	9.12.1969	23.12.1969	15	Dogs	1	Stancombe Wills Glacier	D Wilkins & C Platt
69/18	11.12.1969	24.12.1969	14	Skidoo	1	Hinge Zone	J Carter & N Riley
69/19	14.12.1969	30.12.1969	17	Skidoo	1	Shelf	C Gostick & D MacLennan
Totals for year 1969			269	19	34		
70/1	2.1.1970	13.1.1970	12	Skidoo	1	Shelf	C Gostick, D Sealey
70/2	4.1.1970	19.1.1970	16	Skidoo	1	Hinge Zone	J Carter & N Riley
70/3	12.1.1970	15.1.1970	4	Manhaul	1	Shelf	J Chalmers & D Wilkins
70/4	10.3.1970	18.3.1970	9	Dogs	1	Hinge Zone	G Wright & M Warden
70/5	10.3.1970	31.3.1970	22	Dogs	2	Shelf	M Guyatt & D Peel, M Vallance & I Leith
70/6	6.4.1970	22.4.1970	17	Muskeg	2	Shelf	M Guyatt & D Peel, D Devitt & D Hoy
70/7	19.9.1970	2.10.1970	14	Dogs	2	Bob Pi recce	G Wright & M Taylor, M Vallance & D Peel
70/8	19.9.1970	4.10.1970	16	Dogs	1	Shelf	M Warden & J Nockels then B Cormack
70/9	27.9.1970	20.10.1970	24	Skidoo	1	Shelf	M Guyatt & M Pinder
70/10	28.9.1970	4.10.1970	7	Muskeg	2	Bob Pi recce	D Hoy, G Soar, P Burton, S Bean
70/11	13.10.1970	9.12.1970	58	Muskeg Skidoo	2 1	Ice Cap	D Peel, M Vallance, P Burton, S Bean, D Hoy
70/12	15.10.1970	25.10.1970	11	Dogs	2	Wright Line recce	G Wright & I Smith, M Warden & H Jones (Discovered "The Wright Line" as alternative to deteriorating Bob Pi crossing)

Year/exped.	Depart	Return	Days	Type	Units	Destination	Personnel
70/13	25.10.1970	1.11.1970	8	Manhaul	1	Bob Pi	I Leith & A Clayton or A Gannon
70/14	22.11.1970	1.12.1970	10	Dogs	2	Shelf	D Clark & M Taylor, I Leith & J Gauntlet
70/15	30.11.1970	1.2.1971	64	Aircraft Dogs	2 2	W Shackletons	P Clarkson & M Warden, G Wright & R Wyeth (3rd expedition air lifted to Shackletons by Americans. Lockheed C130 aircraft Clarkson & Wyeth flown to Halley and back out)
70/16	4.12.1970	30.12.1970	27	Dogs	1	Shelf	A Clayton & M Taylor
70/17	14.12.1970	30.12.1970	17	Dogs	1	Shelf	G Soar & K Chappell
Totals for year 1970			336	17	28		
71/1	11.1.1971	16.1.1971	6	Skidoo	1	Shelf	M Guyatt, R Wells, A Gannon
71/2	13.1.1971	20.1.1971	8	Dogs	2	Wright Line recce	M Vallance & M Pinder, B Jarvis, R Chappell replaced I Leith in field
71/3	16.3.1971	23.3.1971	8	Skidoo	2	Shelf	H Stoneham, T Thomas, T Gannon
71/4	16.3.1971	24.3.1971	9	Dogs	2	Wright Line recce	M Warden & P Jones, S Bean & R Patterson
71/5	24.3.1971	30.3.1971	7	Dogs	1	Shelf	R Leigh, H Jones
71/6	30.3.1971	7.4.1971	9	Dogs	1	Shelf	M Taylor & B Blackwell
71/7	5.4.1971	6.4.1971	2	Dogs	1	Shelf	M Vallance, P Brangham
71/8	6.9.1971	12.9.1971	7	Dogs	1	Shelf	M Vallance & A Gannon
71/9	21.9.1971	5.10.1971	15	Dogs Muskeg	2 2	Wright Line	M Warden & P Brangham, H Jones & R Lee, S Bean, H Stoneham, I Bury
71/10	4.10.1971	2.11.1971	30	Muskeg	2	Ice Cap	H Stoneham, K Stewardson, AJ Smith, S Bean
71/11	6.10.1971	14.10.1971	9	Dogs	1	Bob Pi recce	M Taylor & G Devine

Year/exped.	Depart	Return	Days	Type	Units	Destination	Personnel
71/12	14.10.1971	23.11.1971	41	Muskeg	2	Shelf	P Brangham, N Eddleston, J Rushby, A Gannon
71/13	27.10.1971	8.11.1971	13	Dogs	1	Shelf	M Taylor & J Flick
71/14	27.10.1971	14.11.1971	19	Dogs	1	Shelf coast	M Warden & R Loan
71/15	11.11.1971	19.11.1971	9	Manhaul	1	Bob Pi	P Jones, R Lee, T Thomas
71/16	12.11.1971	9.12.1971	28	Dogs	1	Shelf coast	M Vallance & I Bury
71/17	20.11.1971	8.12.1971	19	Manhaul	1	Shelf	B Blackwell & B Cornock
71/18	21.11.1971	9.12.1971	19	Skidoo	1	Shelf coast	A Gannon & J Nockels
71/19	23.11.1971	21.12.1971	29	Dogs	1	Riiser-Larsen Ice Shelf	M Warden, J Flick (Achieved furthest north from Halley 73°15'S 19°30'W)
71/20	24.11.1971	4.12.1971	11	Dogs	1	Shelf	M Taylor & R Paterson
71/21	11.12.1971	25.12.1971	15	Dogs	1	Shelf	G Devine & S Bean
71/22	21.12.1971	29.12.1971	9	Dogs	1	Shelf	P Jones, T Thomas
71/23	30.12.1971	14.1.1972	16	Dogs	2	Hinge Zone	M Warden, H Jones, K Stewardson
Totals for year 1971			338	23	32		
72/1	2.1.1972	15.1.1972	14	Dogs	1	Shelf coast	P Brangham & R Lee
72/2	4.2.1972	9.2.1972	6	Dogs	2	Wright Line recce	J Donaldson & H Stoneham, D Fletcher & I Campbell (One dog team and sledge lost in crevasse - all dogs dead, men ok)
72/3	21.2.1972	4.3.1972	13	Muskeg Dogs	2 / 2	Wright Line salvage party see 72/2	H Stoneham, G Ramage, D Fletcher J Donaldson, I Bury, T Thomas

Year/exped.	Depart	Return	Days	Type	Units	Destination	Personnel
72 / 4	10.3.1972	22.3.1972	13	Dogs	3	Shelf	D Fletcher & D Habgood, J Donaldson & B Jenkins, B Blackwell & T Boyt
72 / 5	28.3.1972	5.4.1972	9	Dogs	2	Shelf	D Fletcher, K Stewardson, R Daynes
72 / 6	10.4.1972	13.4.1972	4	Muskeg	1	Shelf	H Stoneham, P Jones, R Loan
72 / 7	4.9.1972	16.9.1972	13	Muskeg	1	Bob Pi	B Blackwell, D Fletcher, I Bury (investigate lost tractor see 69/11)
72 / 8	25.9.1972	15.10.1972	21	Dogs	2	Shelf	R Daynes, J Donaldson, D Habgood
72 / 9	5.10.1972	18.10.1972	14	Skidoo	1	Shelf	H Stoneham, I Campbell, K Stewardson
72 / 10	16.10.1972	3.11.1972	19	Dogs	2	Shelf	J Donaldson & B Jenkins, D Fletcher & I Campbell
72 / 11	17.10.1972	28.10.1972	12	Skidoo	1	Shelf	P Brangham, G Ramage, G Devine
72 / 12	19.10.1972	4.11.1972	17	Muskeg Skidoo	1 2	Bob Pi	B Blackwell & D Fletcher G Ramage & I Bury (Recovery of International Harvester lost in Nov 69 - see 72/7 & 69/11)
72 / 13	4.11.1972	27.11.1972	24	Dogs	2	Shelf	J Donaldson & R Loan, D Fletcher & A Jackson
72 / 14	6.11.1972	24.11.1972	19	Skidoo	1	Shelf	T Thomas & K Acheson
72 / 15	6.11.1972	25.11.1972	20	Manhaul	1	Bob Pi	P Jones, I Campbell
72 / 16	28.11.1972	7.12.1972	10	Skidoo	1	Shelf	I Bury, N Eddleston, AJ Smith
72 / 17	28.11.1972	14.12.1972	17	Dogs	2	Shelf	J Donaldson, D Fletcher & T Boyt
72 / 18	9.12.1972	16.12.1972	8	Skidoo	1	Shelf	K Acheson, B Blackwell, B Jenkins
Totals for year 1972			253		31		

Appendix 3

Halley Bay Huskies

Despite their beauty and their gentle faces, Huskies are in effect powerful tractors, specially adapted to polar climes, and able to withstand the harshest weather the Antarctic can throw at them. To call them "hardy" is to understate their resources, nevertheless like any dog (or human), if given affection they will respond - some enthusiastically, others cautiously, while a few will remain aloof. It has to be remembered however that with the exception of "Stumpy" (Halley Bay's first Husky), and the small group left over in the late '70's (which were essentially Base pets) the Halley dogs were primarily a means of transport. The animals, like the tractors, were maintained, refuelled, run and then garaged until the next expedition. True, the puppies, which were normally born in the winter months were kept indoors until sufficiently robust to tolerate the outside temperatures, and they were also allowed to wander freely in the summer months, but once they reached *doghood* they were destined to spend the rest of their lives tethered in the open air or in an underground ice kennel. There were the field trips of course, the dogs *raison d'être,* and maybe some dogs anticipated these expeditions with excitement (or perhaps they just wanted freedom) but there could be many months of waiting - a wait that must have been especially tedious and gruelling over the long, cold, dark winters. It was a dog's life you might justifiably say.

Although the dogs were in effect our traction engines and we worked them hard, many doggymen, like myself, became quite attached to particular animals but, regardless of favourites, all were treated the same and that treatment was occasionally harsh and often negligent. We could have done much better for all the animals but we were quite ignorant and ill tutored, each new dog driver learning from "old hands" who themselves had only a smattering of knowledge handed down from the previous inexperienced generation. For instance Huskies needed exercise during their long months of tethering but rarely got it. If not assigned to an expedition, a few lucky dogs enjoyed the treat of a run with a light sledge in the warmer summer period but rarely if ever during the rest of the year, unlucky dogs might stay tethered almost the whole time. They also needed considerably more individual attention than we afforded them. We were naive, untrained, unaware. We used the dogs and then largely ignored them. The Husky loving and racing fraternity would be horrified.

In this environment of harsh usage it should come as no surprise that dogs were "put down", culled, shot when their working life was over - and that such a life was relatively short.

Even so, despite our ignorance, we doggymen had a real soft spot for those wonderful, powerful, reliable, loveable beasts and I feel deeply privileged to have run with Antarctic Huskies.

HALLEY BAY HUSKIES

Key: B - born, X - years at Halley, T - transferred to another base

Name	Dog/Bitch	Origin	'56	'57	'58	'59	'60	'61	'62	'63	'64	'65	'66	'67	'68	'69	'70	'71	'72	'73	'74	'75	'76	'77	'78	'79	'80	'81	Comments and cause of death
Stumpy	B	Norway	-	-	X	X	X	X																					lone pet for 5 yrs - died natural causes - born 55?
Bodach	D	Anvers Island		B	-	-	-	-	X	X	X	X	X	X															put down - senile
Booboo	D	Halley Bay						B	X	X	X	X	X	X	X	X	X	X											culled
Debbie 1	B	Signy Island		B	-	-	-	X	X	X																			lost in sea ice accident with Neville Mann
Eigg	D	Admiralty Bay				B	-	-	X	X	X	X	X	X															eye destroyed in fight - died in surgery
Fay	B	Admiralty Bay		B	-	-	-	-	X	X	X	X	X	X															put down due to illness
Gnat	D	Horseshoe Is	-	-	-	-	-	-	X	X	X																		culled (born '55)
Kate	B	Horseshoe Is	B	-	-	-	-	-	X	X	X																		culled
Kelly 1	D	Halley Bay						B	X	X																			lost in sea ice accident with Neville Mann
Larsen	D	Halley Bay						B	X																				natural causes - possible appendicitis
Macnab	D	Prospect Pt		B	-	-	-	X	X	X																			culled
Muck 2	D	Admiralty Bay				B	-	X	X	X	X	X	X	X															natural causes - hypothermia?
Oscar	D	Halley Bay						B	X	X	X	X	X	X	X	X													culled
Pam 2	B	Admiralty Bay		B	-	-	-	-	X	X	X	X																	ran away on expedition
Rhum	D	Admiralty Bay				B	-	-	X	X	X	X	X	X	X	X													put down - osteoarthritis
Shep	D	Hope Bay	-	-	-	-	-	-	X	X	X																		culled (born '53)
Tina	B	Admiralty Bay		B	-	-	-	-	X	X	X	X	X	X															put down on expedition - paralysis of back legs
Vere	D	Anvers Island		B	-	-	-	-	X	X	X																		culled
Wendy	B	Admiralty Bay		B	-	-	-	-	X	X	X																		culled
Zork	D	Halley Bay						B	X	X																			lost in sea ice accident with Neville Mann

Name	Dog/Bitch	Origin	'56	'57	'58	'59	'60	'61	'62	'63	'64	'65	'66	'67	'68	'69	'70	'71	'72	'73	'74	'75	'76	'77	'78	'79	'80	'81	Comments and cause of death
Barney 1	D	Halley Bay							B																					natural causes - heart failure
Bostick	D	Halley Bay							B	X																			lost in sea ice accident with Neville Mann
Rastus 2	D	Halley Bay							B	X	X	X	X	X	X	X	X	X											culled
Rolf	D	Halley Bay							B	X	X	X	X	X	X	X	X												put down due to illness
Royal	D	Halley Bay							B	X	X	X	X	X	X	X													culled
Slod	D	Halley Bay							B	X	X	X																	natural causes
Nanuk	D	Hope Bay						B	-	-	X	X	X																ran away on expedition
Nuga	D	Greenland								B	-	X	X	X	X	X													put down - arthritis
Pop	D	Hope Bay						B	-	X	X	X	X	X															culled
Raq	D	Hope Bay					B	-	-	X	X	X	X	X															put down on expedition - became incurably ill
Skye	D	Hope Bay						B	-	X	X	X	X	X															culled
Stroma	D	Hope Bay								B	-	X	X	X	X	X	X												culled
Wifred	D	Hope Bay								B	-	X	X	X	X	X	X												died in sleep - natural causes
Balasuaq	D	Greenland							B	-	-	X	X	X	X	X	X	X	X										culled
Barajo	D	Hope Bay						B	-	X	X	X	X																death not recorded
Barra	D	Hope Bay							B	-	X	X	X	X	X	X													culled
Bitter	D	Hope Bay				B	-	-	-	X	X	X																	put down on expedition - severe arthritis
Emma	B	Cape Reclus				B	-	-	-	X	X	X																	culled - senile
Jukal	D	Hope Bay				B	-	-	-	X																			culled
Mild	D	Hope Bay						B	-	X	X	X	X																culled
Satan 2	D	Hope Bay						B	-	X	X																		died - possibly gorged to death on 20 meat bars
Snowy 2	B	Hope Bay						B	X	X	X	X	X	X															culled
Staffa	D	Hope Bay						B	-	X	X	X	X	X															culled

Name	Dog/Bitch	Origin	'56	'57	'58	'59	'60	'61	'62	'63	'64	'65	'66	'67	'68	'69	'70	'71	'72	'73	'74	'75	'76	'77	'78	'79	'80	'81	Comments and cause of death
Whisky 2	D	Greenland					B	-	-	-	X	X	X	X															natural causes on expedition - heart attack?
Borga	B	Deception Is									B	X	X	X															put down - faulty heart
Changi	D	Halley Bay										B	X	X	X	X	X	X											fell down crevasse in hinge zone with whole team
Dove	B	Deception Is										B	X	X	X	X	X												culled
Esk	D	Deception Is										B	X	X	X	X	X	X	X										fell down crevasse in hinge zone with whole team
Fedu	D	Halley Bay											B	X	X	X	X	X	X										culled
Frosty	B	Hope Bay								B	-	-	X	X	X	X	X	X	X										culled
Ham	D	Halley Bay											B	X	X	X	X	X	X	T									transferred to Stonington 73
Japhet	D	Halley Bay												B															savaged by bitch - no ID no. allocated
Luqa	D	Halley Bay											B	X	X	X	X	X	X										fell down crevasse in hinge zone with whole team
Medina	B	Deception Is										B	X																ran away on expedition - fell in Bob Pi. crevasse
Seletar	D	Halley Bay											B	X	X	X	X	X	X	X									culled
Sharjah	D	Halley Bay											B	X	X	X	X	X	X	X	T								transferred to Stonington 73
Shem	D	Halley Bay											B	X	X	X	X	X	X	T									transferred to Stonington 73
Teifi	B	Deception Is											B	X	X	X	X												transferred to Scott Base in exchange for Umiak 2
Tengah	D	Halley Bay											B	X	X	X	X	X	X	X	T								transferred to Stonington 73
Wensen	D	Deception Is											B	X	X	X	X	X	X										fell down crevasse in hinge zone with whole team
Chalky	B	Hope Bay								B	-	-	X	X															culled
Chroma	D	Adelaide Is											B	X															natural causes - septic heart valve
Colic	D	Adelaide Is											B	X	X	X	X	X	X										culled
Dusty 3	B	Deception Is											B	X	X	X	X	X											culled
Flossie	B	Deception Is											B	X	X														natural causes - possible hypothermia after whelping
Francoise	B	Deception Is											B	X	X	X	X												culled

Name	Dog/Bitch	Origin	'56	'57	'58	'59	'60	'61	'62	'63	'64	'65	'66	'67	'68	'69	'70	'71	'72	'73	'74	'75	'76	'77	'78	'79	'80	'81	Comments and cause of death
Jill 2	B	Deception Is											B	X															culled
Jock 2	D	Deception Is											B	X	X	X	X	X	X	X									culled
Kolya	D	Halley Bay												B															put down - rheumatism and heart trouble
Lady 3	B	Deception Is											B	X	X	X													transferred to Scott Base in exchange for Umiak 2
Lassie 2	B	Deception Is											B	X	X	X	X	X	X										culled
Lin	B	Adelaide Is											B	X	X														culled
Lister	D	Deception Is											B	X	X	X	X												put down - acute pain - complications after surgery
Lobo 2	D	Deception Is											B	X	X	X	X	X	X										fell down crevasse in hinge zone with whole team
Lotus 2	B	Deception Is											B	X	X														natural causes - possible hypothermia after whelping
Michelle	B	Deception Is											B	X	X	X	X	X	X	X									culled
Mitral	D	Adelaide Is											B	X	X	X	X	X	X										fell down crevasse in hinge zone with whole team
Mitya	D	Halley Bay												B	X	X	X	T											transferred to Stonington 73
Moo	B	Deception Is											B	X															fell in crevasse near Mobster Creek
Rover 2	D	Deception Is											B	X	X	X	X												put down - severely injured after fight in dog tunnel
Steno	D	Adelaide Is											B	X															killed - savaged by bitch
Tricia	B	Deception Is											B	X	X	X													culled
Trixie	B	Deception Is											B	X	X	X	X												put down on expedition after severe foot injury
Abdul	D	Halley Bay													B	X	X	X	X	X	T								transferred to Stonington 73
April	B	Halley Bay													B	X	X	X	X	X	T								transferred to Hope Bay
Arwen	B	Halley Bay													B														no record - believed died before ID no allocated
Boby	B	Halley Bay													B	X	X	X	X										fell down crevasse in hinge zone with whole team
Bompur	D	Halley Bay													B														put down after savaging by a bitch
Bophur	D	Halley Bay													B	X	X	X	X										fell down crevasse in hinge zone with whole team

- 217 -

Name	Dog/Bitch	Origin	'56	'57	'58	'59	'60	'61	'62	'63	'64	'65	'66	'67	'68	'69	'70	'71	'72	'73	'74	'75	'76	'77	'78	'79	'80	'81	Comments and cause of death
Dad	D	Halley Bay													B	X	X	X	X										culled
Eleanor	B	Halley Bay													B	X	X	X											culled
Elsa	B	Halley Bay													B	X	X	X	X	X									culled
Evie	B	Halley Bay													B	X	X	X	X	X									culled
Frodo	D	Halley Bay													B	X	X	X	X	X	X								culled
Gandalf	D	Halley Bay													B	X	X	X	X										fell down crevasse in hinge zone with whole team
Gollum	D	Halley Bay													B	X													natural causes - wasted away & died on expedition
Inga	B	Halley Bay													B	X	X	X	X										culled
Josie	B	Halley Bay													B	X	X	X											natural causes - lungs full of blood
Merry	D	Halley Bay													B	X	X												natural causes - died on expedition - Intestinal trouble
Pat	B	Halley Bay													B	X	X	X	X	X									culled
Pippin	D	Halley Bay													B	X	X	X	X	X									culled
Ratti	D	Halley Bay													B	X	X	X	X	T									transferred to Stonington 73
Rosie 3	B	Halley Bay													B														culled
Skipper	D	Halley Bay													B	X													put down - bowel injury
Umiak 2	D	Scott Base											B	-	X	X	X	X	X										culled (birth year estimated)
Zita	B	Halley Bay													B	X	X	X											culled
Audrey	B	Halley Bay													B	X	X	X											put down- injured fell down gash shaft
Bunny	D	Halley Bay													B	X	X	T											transferred to South Georgia - date estimated
Chey 2	D	Halley Bay													B	X	X	X	X	T									transferred to Stonington 73
Craven	D	Halley Bay													B	X	X	X	X	T									transferred to Stonington 73
Ivan	D	Halley Bay													B														natural causes - no reason given
Mavis	B	Halley Bay													B	T													transferred to Adelaide Island 70

- 218 -

Name	Dog/Bitch	Origin	Record ('56–'81)	Comments and cause of death
Nancy	B	Halley Bay	B X X X	culled
Tuesday	B	Halley Bay	B X X X T	transferred to Stonington 73
Ari	D	Halley Bay	B T	transferred to Stonington 71
Arkid	D	Halley Bay	B X X X	culled
Duek	B	Halley Bay	B T	transferred to Stonington 71
Fin	D	Halley Bay	B X X X	culled
Freckles	B	Halley Bay	B X X X	culled
Kalaleq	D	Greenland	B X X X	culled (birth year estimated)
Kunute	D	Greenland	B X X X X T	transferred to Stonington 73 (birth year estimated)
Naf	D	Halley Bay	B T	transferred to Stonington 71
Quebec	B	Halley Bay	B X	culled
Woolfe	D	Halley Bay	B X X T	transferred to Stonington 73
Beda	B	Halley Bay	B	natural causes - pneumonia
Beorn	D	Halley Bay	B X X	death not recorded
Brae	D	Halley Bay	B X X X X X X X X X X	culled
Helix	D	Halley Bay	B X T	transferred to Stonington 73
Isolde	B	Halley Bay	B X X	death not recorded
Kirstie 2	B	Halley Bay	B X T	transferred to Stonington 73
Muff	D	Halley Bay	B X X X X X X X X	put down - severely arthritic
Strider	D	Halley Bay	B X T	transferred to Stonington 73
Nadine	B	Rothera	B - - - - X	natural causes - stomach ulcers (birth estimated)
Ralph	D	Rothera	B - - - X X X T	transferred to Rothera 81 (birth year estimated)
Tom 3	D	Rothera	B - - - X X X T	transferred to Rothera 81 (birth year estimated)

Dog statistics for the entire dog years

Arrivals

total huskies that lived at Halley*	135
dogs	86
bitches	49
huskies born at Halley*	68
imported from other BAS bases	59
from Greenland	6
from Norway	1
from Scott Base (New Zealand base)	1
greatest number at one period (Jan 69)	app 55

(The actual total figure for 1969 calcuates at 69 but early culling and late whelping meant that the number was less at any given time.)

Departures

died of natural causes	16
infirm or injured and put down	17
died in crevasses	11
lost on sea ice	4
ran away and not seen again	3
pup savaged by bitch	2
died under surgery	1
gorged to death?	1
transferred to other bases	25
culled	52
not recorded	_4
	136

It may be noted that 135 dogs lived at Halley but 136 departed! That one animal discrepancy is the bitch Medina who ran away and then fell into a crevasse in the Bob Pi Crossing - so she earns two departures.

The Naming of Huskies

Although choosing good names should have been important to avoid confusion and be clearly heard, many names seemed not to have had this scrutiny. Françoise, Nadine, Beorg and the like do not call well. Some "ordinary" dog names were inevitably duplicated or even triplicated over the years so to avoid confusion in records (and especially in the breeding programme) numbers were appended to their name eg. Snowy 2 and Rover 3. These suffixes were not used in practice as there were never two of any name on one base at the same time, the namesakes being either be at another base or more probably deceased.

On all bases, dog litters were usually given themed or linked names such as Pip, Squeak & Wilfred; Snap, Crackle & Pop; Ham, Shem & Japhet; but siblings were often split up and sent to different bases, thus a new doggyman might sometimes wonder about the choice of a particular name if only one of a set were evident on base. Of the above mentioned animals only Wilfred, Pop, Ham and Shem worked at Halley.

There were drinkers' sets such as, Mild & Bitter; Gin, Whisky & Rum. There were geographical groups such as the two sets of Scottish island brothers Barra, Staffa, Stroma & Skye and Rhum, Eigg & Muck, and there were the more esoteric such as the six RAF air base boys Changi, Luqa, Seletar, Sharjah, Tengah & Fedu. There was also, perhaps inevitably, a plethora of Tolkein names (from several bitches) which inevitably led to the team name "The Hobbits". Often names were selected by the "dog man" but sometimes suggestions were invited and then a vote (and sweepstake) taken on the offerings.

Appendix 4

Field Rations

One box contained rations sufficient for two men for ten days.

Meat bar	20 x 5 oz blocks
Biscuits	32 packets of 6 or 24 of 8
Soup pkts	10 x 1.5 pints
Onions dried	8 oz
Chocolate, plain	12 bars
Chocolate, milk	12 bars
Tea	48 bags
Salt	2 x 2 oz drums
Sugar cubes	4 x 1 lb packets
Porridge	1 x 3 lb packet
Cocoa	1 x 12 oz tin
Milk powder	2 x 1 lb tins
Potato powder	1 x 7 oz packet
Bacon	1 x 16 oz tin
Butter	6 x 1 lb tins
Marmite	1 x 2 oz tube
Cheese	2 x 12 oz tins
Vitamin capsules	100
Tin openers	2

To the above the following are useful additions:

Herbs	1 packet
Curry	4 or 8 oz poly bottle
Cayenne pepper	Small amount.
Salt	2 or 4 oz poly bottle ,
Loose sugar	milk tin full
Jam	

Appendix 5

PO Bag and P Bag   (Post office bag and personal bag)

Apart from rescue equipment and skis, each field man was issued
with a post office bag containing:

1	air bed	1	sheepskin
1 pr	duvet trousers	1	sheet sleeping bag
1	duvet jacket	1	inner sleeping bag
1 pr	slippers	1	outer sleeping bag
1 pr	anklets (if available)	1	sleeping bag cover
1 pr	sheepskin boots (ditto)	1	blanket strap

Assuming the field man was wearing:

sledging anorak	mukluk boots
windproof trousers	2 pr mukluk inners
sweater (wool)	2 pr socks
trousers (wool)	leather gauntlets
vest & Briefs	duffel gloves
wool shirt (long sleeves)	woollen gloves
balaclava	silk gloves
sun glasses & goggles	

[fleece jacket & trousers were new and under test by some
of us]

Spare clothing that should be added:

1	base anorak or wind proofs (1 set to 2 men)		
1 pr	mountain boots or 1 pr mukluks + duffel inners		
1	sweater	1 pr	Briefs
1	shirt	4 pr	Socks
1 pr	leather gauntlets	1 pr	Pyjamas
2 pr	duffel gloves	6	handkerchiefs
3 pr	woollen gloves	1	headband
3 pr	chamois gloves	2 pr	sunglasses
1 pr	Long johns	2 pr	goggles

Appendix 6

Glossary

13/90	The field depot 180 miles along the reconnaissance route from the Therons to the Shackletons and situated at the north east extremity of that route.
13/117	The field depot 234 miles along the reconnaissance route from the Therons to the Shackletons. The furthest point reached by the tractors in 1967.
Avtur	Aviation turbine kerosene - a pretty dirty, non-freezing paraffin that powered the big tractors and generators and clogged up our primus stove burners.
BAS	The British Antarctic Survey - department of the National Environmental Research Council (NERC).
Bob Pi Crossing	Safest known route across the Hinge Zone, pioneered by Alan Precious and party in 1961 but accidentally named after Bob Lee and Pi Jarman who made the first tractor traverse.
Cathedral Cairn	Specially tall snow cairn at the head of the Slessor Glacier built during the Shackleton recce to hopefully assist an expedition the following year. It remained eminently visible.
Chesterfield	The spire at Chesterfield Church (Derbyshire) was made of unseasoned timber. As it dried, it warped and the spire now famously has a leaning twist.
Crampons	Metal sole with spikes that can be lashed to a boot for secure grip on hard ice.

Crossroads	The Depot at the top of the Bob Pi Slope. The start of the plateau ice and routes to the Shackletons (SE), Therons (S), Heimfrontfjella and Vestfjella (E) and the coast (W) as well as the Bob Pi and Halley (N). Initially it was known as Depot 36 but was renamed when its number was no longer in sequence with route flags.
Dead man	Any object buried to form a secure anchor for a rope or ship's warp.
Deep soft	Deep, fresh, usually sticky, snow. Hated by dogs and drivers alike
Depot	Dumps of food, fuel and equipment were made at various points in an expedition. Their content depended on their purpose which might be any of the following:
Depot (main)	Tractor & stove fuel plus food and equipment laid in advance to support a tractor (and possibly dog) expedition. These could be quite large. 13/117, the contents of which were later moved to Depot Dad in the Shackletons, contained two Nansen sledges, sets of dog harnesses and traces, several hundred metres of climbing rope, a tent, 120 gallons of fuel, 13 manfood boxes, 4 boxes of dog food, 2,700 cigarettes, a veritable library of paperbacks, 22 toilet rolls (needed), 20 tablets of soap (not needed), 21 packs of Persil (definitely not needed), 2 field radios plus a long list of spares for everything, even clothing and 108 bars of chocolate! It would have been possible to deposit four men and eighteen dogs by light aircraft and they would have wanted for nothing!

	Depot Dad was found and used by Graham Wright and party in 1970.
Depot (fuel)	Tractor fuel laid on outward journey, usually every 100 miles to refuel the return trip.
Depot (sledging)	Ten day supplies of stove fuel, man food and dog food boxes laid every 50 miles by home bound tractors for the dog teams returning later. This ration was excessively generous as one could normally cover the fifty miles in three moderate days. It led to much raiding of otherwise unneeded food boxes for sugar, chocolate and soup which left almost full boxes in an unusable condition for future trips.
Dog Spans	The permanent lines of wire rope staked to the ice at Halley to which individual dog traces were attached, giving each dog its private space. There were about six wires, each with a dozen or so dogs.
Elsan	The name of a chemical toilet, as well as an old motor toboggan.
Fid	A man who has over-wintered on one of BAS's Antarctic bases.
Fidlet	A new Fid yet to complete a winter in Antarctica.
Fids	The Falkland Islands Dependency Survey (later BAS) or plural of fid.
GA	The abbreviation for "general assistant" but in reality GAs quickly earned defined responsibilities such as chief dog man, tractor mechanic, field logistics and equipment. This to the extent that some of we GAs rather resented the somewhat demeaning full title while proudly declaring

the initials. However in addition to our specific responsibilities we did assist almost everyone else on base in their work. GAs were often referred to as Gash 'Ands but not to be confused with the "gash 'and" job of cleaning that everyone had to undertake on a rota.

Gash (i) Rubbish or waste. Hence being "on gash" was the regular duty of thoroughly cleaning the public rooms, topping up the water melt tanks, assisting the cook and generally keeping the base habitable. It also included the "gash run" of dumping or burning accumulated rubbish some distance from the base.

Gash (ii) Spare (or unclaimed) commodities of any sort: timber, rope, clothing, food (not to be confused with waste food destined for the gash bin in the loo!).

Glare ice A hard glassy surface on the snow.

Golly's Castle Specially large snow cairn at the head of the Slessor Glacier built during the Shackleton recce to assist the return of Noble and Skidmore, also to hopefully assist an expedition the following year.

Golly's Folly The sledge mounted caboose or caravan used on the Shackletons tractor traverse.

Grillage village Nickname applied to Halley 2, (Halley Bay 1967 New Base in old jargon). The name derived from the steel grill or mesh that was laid under every hut to give a flat working surface and attempt to spread the load on the snow.

Heimfrontfjella	Mountain range in the Norwegian claimed territory Dronning Maud Land and 350 miles east of Halley Bay. First visited by Ardus and Johnson in 1961.
Hinge Zone	The ten mile wide region of heavy crevassing between the shelf ice and the inland ice resulting mainly from the hinging of the shelf as it rose and fell with the tide, but also the sudden change from a down hill slope to horizontal as the ice sheet lifted off the land to float on the sea.
Ice shelf	The Antarctic ice sheet, a few hundred to a few thousand metres thick flows outwards and downwards to the coast under its own weight. At the coast it cannot simply stop but carries on spreading. Being less dense than the sea water it floats and in a sheltered or confined bay can remain attached to the land ice for thousands of years, its extremities periodically breaking off as icebergs.
IGY	The International Geophysical Year of 1957/58 when many nations set up research projects throughout the world.
Lampwick	25 mm wide heavy duty cotton tape used for the best dog harnesses.
Llareggub	Name given to the snow cairn at Point Touché. Read backwards it describes what we felt we had achieved!
Mukluks	Canvas boots with simple lacing and easy to put on with plenty of room for socks and liners.
Névé	Good ice, part way between snow and hard glacier ice.

Night trace	Length of thin wire rope to which individual dog traces were attached giving dogs more personal space at night.
Norah Batty	Character in a television show who always had wrinkled stockings.
Nunatak	Rock summit projecting above an ice sheet. Because the lower mountain slopes cannot be seen the mountains look to be "up to their necks" in ice.
Nutrican	Compressed meat bars for the huskies.
Nutty	General name for chocolate, whatever the flavour.
Old base	Halley 1, comprising the original IGY hut, the 1961 accommodation hut and the 1964 office block. All at different levels within the ice. In January 67 the office block was almost on the surface but the IGY was some fifteen metres below.
Payload	The weight of personnel, expedition equipment and depot materials but excluding the tractors, cargo sledges and fuel for the journey.
Point Touché	80° 31′ S the furthest point reached by Noble & Skidmore on the Shackleton reconnaissance in January 1968.
Prussiks	Metal camming clamps that when attached to a harness and foot loops permit a rope to be climbed.
Recce	Abbreviation for reconnoitre and reconnaissance.
Sastrugi	Wind sculpted lumps of hard packed snow
Scradge	Main meal of the day whether on base or in the field and regardless of ingredients or quality, but perhaps more particularly the

	unappetising meat bar stew of camp menus.
Shacks	The Shackleton Mountains, named for Sir Ernest Shackleton and first visited by Sir Vivian Fuchs' party in 1956. In my account the term applies at first to the whole range but then more specifically to the Eastern Shackletons as our focus became directed that way. The Eastern Shacks were later named Pioneer Escarpment, though none of our team was included amongst the honoured pioneers.
Shelf Ice	See "Ice shelf"
Skijor line	Skijoring was being towed on skis behind two or three dogs or a tractor and quite exhilarating too, but the skijor line on a dog sledge was a thin rope that was attached to the front of the sledge with a loop handle at the other end and of the right length for the driver to hold. This meant that when the dogs ran faster than the driver could walk he could be pulled by holding the line and the handlebar. With no line this would have been unbalancing and very strenuous on the one holding arm.
Smoko	Navy term for the morning or afternoon break. On base fresh hot bread rolls or cakes were usually served with the tea or coffee.
Spans	See Dog spans
Spirit of Ecstasy	The silver figurine that adorns the bonnet of Rolls Royce cars.
Squadcall	A "single side band" two way field radio made by Racal. (Please don't ask what single side band is!)

Therons	A mountain range 250 miles south of Halley Bay named after the "MV Theron", the ship that deposited the Trans Antarctic Expedition in 1956. The range was first explored by Samuel, Wornham, Johnson and Brook in 1966.
Thumper	A short length of thick rope with a spliced loop handle, used for chastising dogs!
Tottans	Correctly the Tottanfjella (fjella = mountains), the western end of the Heimfrontfjella. Named after the "MV Tottan" the ship that established Halley Bay in 1956.
Tufnel	A slippery very hard wearing laminate used for the soles of sledge runners.
Turk's Head	A decorative knot reminiscent of a turban.
Vestfjella	A mountain range 330 miles north east of Halley, first explored by Russell and Wild in 1965.
Whiteout	Condition when total cloud cover eliminates all surface details and the horizon cannot be discerned. "Deep whiteout" - my own term - the totally disorientating conditions of whiteout with fog.
Yellow ice	A sign that man (or dog) has stopped momentarily to "admire the view".